Julius Lester—author of *Look Out Whitey! Black Power's Gon' Get Your Mama, Search for the New Land,* and the forthcoming *The Seventh Son: An Anthology of the Writings of W. B. DuBois*—is a man of many parts: columnist, folk singer, radio personality, and photographer. He has written two juveniles: *To Be A Slave,* which was the 1968 Newbery Medal runner-up, and *Black Folktales.* His writings have appeared in *The Guardian, Broadsides, Liberation,* and *Sing Out.* On WBAI, the Pacifica Foundation station in New York, his program has served as a forum for black viewpoints. He has also cut two albums for Vanguard Records.

# REVOLUTIONARY NOTES

# REVOLUTIONARY NOTES

**JULIUS LESTER**

GROVE PRESS, INC., NEW YORK

Library of Congress Catalog Card Number: 79-84215

First Evergreen Black Cat Edition, 1970

First Printing

Manufactured in the United States of America

# CONTENTS

# INTRODUCTION

REVOLUTIONARIES are not born. They are made by feeling the pain of everyone who has lived and suffered. Why some take this pain as their own and others do not, I don't know. For some, it is impossible to eat a meal and not feel angry because everyone is not eating. For most, it is not only possible, but also amazingly easy to live without the slightest spasm over another's pain. The revolutionary is he who has reached that stage of psychosocial evolution where the alleviation of his own pain is secondary to alleviating the pain of others. Unlike the Christian missionary, the Florence Nightingale, or the liberal do-gooder, the revolutionary recognizes that to attempt to alleviate the pain of individuals alone is to become engaged in unending acts of frustration. There are too many individuals in pain to attend to them individually. People are oppressed en masse, not separately. They can only be freed en masse. Thus, the revolutionary is concerned with a total change in a society's institutions, for it is the institutions which shape the individuals. At the same time, the revolutionary knows that to change the institutions he must change himself. He and his comrades must become new men, for it is from new men that the new institutions will come which, in turn, will create the new society.

It is toward that concept of the New Man and the new society that these essays are presented. The first part of the book presents essays on the peace movement, the death of Che Guevara, the International War Crimes Tribunal, and the revolutionary. The second part presents what I consider to be the most relevant of the weekly columns I have written for *The Guardian* since the fall of 1967. Sometimes it will appear as if a later essay contradicts something I wrote a few months earlier. I am more concerned that I always write with honesty rather than consistency. To change one's mind is a sign of weakness only to one who equates consistency with strength.

There are many to whom I am indebted in my personal journey toward becoming that most human of all men—the revolutionary. Among them are Rap Brown, with his integrity, total commitment, and love; Kris Dymond, with her gentleness, lack of illusions, her love, and her voice on the telephone; David Gahr, who is like an older brother, teaching me how to fight the thieves for every penny and then some; the people of North Vietnam and Cuba, in whom I saw the New Man made manifest; Fidel Castro, with his humanity, joy at being alive, his energy and his suspicion of me and my cameras; Worth Long, for being; and always, the young, black and white, who know what must be done.

This book is dedicated to Joan, whom I often confuse

with myself, because the longer we live with each other, the more difficult it is for me to know where I leave off and she begins. That is as it should be.

*Julius Lester*
JANUARY 27, 1969

To Joan

who is so much a part
of my Being that to call her
wife is to dehumanize her
and vulgarize our relationship.

So I will call her Joan
because the sound of that name
reverberates from every word
I have written and every breath
of my Being which is also

Joan

# PART ONE

## PROTEST AND RESISTANCE

TO protest is to speak out against, to let it be known that you do not like a certain action of another.

To protest is an act of intellectual commitment. It is to say, "Sir, I protest" when you are slapped in the face . . .

To protest is to play a game. You go to a demonstration, listen to speeches, wave signs, and go home to see if you got on television.

There are many toys in the game of protest.

There is the picket line. Originally a picket line was formed by striking workers to keep strikebreakers out. If anyone tried to cross that picket line, the strikers tried to kill him. Today you get a permit from the police to picket . . .

There is no protest if permission must be sought and rules abided by. We have allowed the form that our protest takes to be defined for us by those whom we protest against. Thus, our protest is drained of its power because we do not have the power to make our protest effective.

We think the war in Vietnam is being waged only

against the Vietnamese, but we are its victims, too. It is our own deaths we protest, but we haven't realized it. It is not a war against "the Vietnamese people." It is a war against us and the little humanity we have remaining. Too little humanity we have remaining. Too little humanity, because we are no longer outraged at what is being done to us.

If we were, we would resist.

To resist is to say No! without qualification or explanation.

To resist is not only to say I Won't Go. It is to say, I'll make sure nobody else goes, either.

To resist is to pit Life as you define it against Life as they define it and to do all that is necessary to see that their definition is destroyed in all of its parts.

To resist is not to go to jail when sentenced, but only when caught and surrounded and there is no other choice but death.

To resist is to make the President afraid to leave the White House because he will be spat upon wherever he goes to tell his lies, because his limousine will find the street filled with tacks and thousands of people who will surge around it, smashing the windows and rocking the car until it is turned on its side.

Have we forgotten? The man is a murderer.

It is us he is killing.

To resist is to realize that your own life is at stake at this very moment.

To resist is to become alive, truly alive for the first time. It is to say not only will I not accept what you are doing, I will stop you from doing it. No one shall sleep peacefully again until you cease, desist, and abdicate.

To resist is to say if the parents of Vietnam weep for

their children then the parents of America shall weep for theirs.

If the people of Vietnam are unable to harvest the crop without fear, to live their lives without being shrouded by the shadow of death, then no American shall harvest his crop without fear, no American shall live outside the shadow of death.

To protest is to dislike the inhumanity of another.

To resist is to stop inhumanity and affirm your own humanity.

One does not protest murder.

One apprehends the murderer and deals with him accordingly.

FIRST PUBLISHED IN THE *Vietnam Summer News*, CAMBRIDGE, MASS., AUGUST 4, 1967

## CHE IS ALIVE—ON EAST 103rd STREET

THEY say that comrade Che is dead. I do not know, but if it is true it is not surprising. All men die, and comrade Che was a man. A bullet does not ask the name of the person toward whom it is being projected. And no man is immune from the effects that a bullet is designed to have.

They say that comrade Che is dead and his death is supposed to mean that the poor and the dispossessed will return to silent discontent, will relinquish the dream of reclaiming their lives and their lands.

It is easy to see why they think this. They always think about one man. They think, Oh how different it would be IF John Kennedy had not been struck down. They think, Oh how different race relations would be IF Abraham Lincoln had not been struck down. Therefore, it is logical for them to think that things will be different now that Major Ernesto Che Guevara is dead.

But it is not important that comrade Che is dead. It is important only that he lived, as that is all that is important for each of us. Death is not a body being flown out of the hills on the runners of a helicopter. Death is not a body placed on display for reporters to view. Death is a life that was not lived. Such cannot be said of comrade Che.

One need only look at the face of comrade Che and the face of Lyndon Johnson to know who represents Life and who represents Death. Even the most reactionary person cannot resist the gentleness and the beauty in the face of comrade Che. Throughout Cuba there are huge posters bearing pictures of him with the caption: "THE JOB OF A REVOLUTIONARY IS TO MAKE THE REVOLUTION." That is, the job of any man is to give Life.

But they do not understand the life-giving beauty of making revolution. If one takes the absolute position that violence is evil, then one cannot understand the difference in the faces of comrade Che, Fidel and the Vietnamese when compared with those of Lyndon Johnson, Dean Rusk and the American G.I. Where is the gentleness in those faces? Where the beauty? Where the love? But they kill because Life threatens them. The revolutionary kills because Death threatens him.

It does not matter that comrade Che is dead. In his message to the second meeting of the Tri-Continental, he spoke of the necessity of creating two, three, many Vietnams. It was understood that by so saying, he recognized that this meant there must be two, three, many Ernesto Che Guevaras.

I can only smile at their celebration on the death of Ernesto Che Guevara. They cannot understand. Several times a year they have reported his death. At one time Fidel was supposed to have had him executed. Each time I could only smile, for what did it matter? To destroy comrade Che, they will have to destroy all of us—the dispossessed—and this they cannot do.

Comrade Che understood this as any revolutionary does, for he ended his message to the Tri-Continental by saying: "Wherever death may surprise us, it will be welcome, provided that this, our battle cry, reaches some receptive ear, that another hand be extended to take up our weapons, and that other men come forward to intone our funeral dirge with the staccato of machine guns and new cries of battle and victory."

In Valle Grande, Bolivia, a body lies. They say that it is Major Ernesto Che Guevara. The body might have that name as an identifying tag but comrade Che is alive—on East 103rd Street.

PUBLISHED IN THE *Westside News* (NEW YORK),
OCTOBER 19, 1967

# JUDGMENT IN STOCKHOLM

IN the first week of May, 1967, the International War Crimes Tribunal met in Stockholm, Sweden, to hear evidence and render judgment on the U.S. role in the war in Vietnam. The Tribunal was conceived in the fall of 1966 by Bertrand Russell and was to have one primary function: to condemn the U.S. for the war in Vietnam.

In Lord Russell's opening statement to the Tribunal, he stated: "In Vietnam we have done what Hitler did in Europe. We shall suffer the degradation of Nazi Germany unless we act . . . It is overdue that those without power sit in judgment over those who have it. This is the test we must meet, alone if need be. We are responsible before history."

To accomplish its task, the Tribunal brought together some of the great intellectual minds of the West—Jean-Paul Sartre, Simone de Beauvoir, Isaac Deutscher, as well as such European radicals as Lelio Basso, Italian Socialist; Vladimir Dedijer, former Yugoslav partisan; and Mehmet Ali Aybar, Turkish Socialist.

From America came Dave Dellinger, Carl Oglesby, and Courtland Cox, who sat in for Stokely Carmichael.

From the Far East came Ali Kasuri, chief prosecutor of Pakistan; Amado Hernandez, former Huk and poet laureate of the Philippines, and a distinguished delegation of Japanese activists and lawyers. And from Cuba came Melba Hernandez, a national heroine and comrade of Fidel from the early beginnings of the Cuban Revolution in the Sierra Maestra.

These were the people who sat for eight days listening to the evidence that had been collected by the four investigating teams sent to North Vietnam, and the evidence was overwhelming. For the first time, it was proven conclusively that the U.S. was systematically bombing schools, churches, hospitals, hamlets, cities, and dikes. It was brought out that the U.S. was using a new kind of antipersonnel bomb—i.e., a bomb designed to kill people rather than cause property damage—the steel-pellet bomb.

It was also brought out that the nature of the war makes it different from any war previously waged. The bombing of North Vietnam is aimed at the psychosocial structure of the country, not at military targets. This accounts for the predominant targets being schools, churches, villages, women, and children. This was made even more clear when one witness read from the Air Force ROTC manual, *Fundamentals of Aerospace Weapons Systems:*

"For purposes of target study, the psychosocial structure of a nation or people is often reduced to terms of morale, because morale is something that can be sensed, observed and influenced . . . Some of the conventional targets for morale attacks have been water supplies, food supplies, housing areas, transportation centers, and industrial sites.

The objectives of these attacks in the past have been to dispel the people's belief in the invincibility of their forces, to create unrest, to reduce the output of the labor force, to cause strikes, sabotage, riots, fear, panic, hunger, and passive resistance to the government, and to create a general feeling that the war should be terminated."

All of this important information and more was heard at the Tribunal, yet few people in America or Europe are aware that there even was a Tribunal, not to mention the nature of the evidence collected by the Tribunal. The press simply blacked out most news about the Tribunal, as it was supposed to do by its very nature. Many Third World political activists viewed the Tribunal as did a diplomat from Mali, who said, "What is the Tribunal going to do? Give Johnson four years in jail?"

This was the political reality. What could the Tribunal do?

Sartre recognized this in his opening statement when he said: "What a strange tribunal: a jury and no judge. It is true; we are only a jury. We have neither the power to condemn, nor the power to acquit, anyone. Therefore, no prosecution. We, the jury, at the end of the session will have to pronounce on the charges: are they well founded or not? But the judges are everywhere. They are the people of the world, and particularly the American people. It is for them that we are working."

The Tribunal's judgment was, of course, that the U.S. was guilty of aggression in Vietnam, that the U.S. was guilty of bombing civilians in North Vietnam. Having said it, what was said? The judgment had not changed the political reality, which was the war in Vietnam. The steel-pellet bombs and napalm were being dropped as the

Tribunal met and they are being dropped now. Yet the feeling at the close of the Tribunal was one of self-satisfaction by most of its members.

When Vladimir Dedijer closed the session on May 8, the audience in Stockholm's Folkets Hus rose to its feet and applauded for a half-hour as members of the Tribunal hugged each other on the stage. The next day Folkets Hus was empty except for the few members of the Swedish committee of the Tribunal who worked at clearing out the accumulation of documents. The Tribunal members themselves had returned to their respective homes and jobs in Paris, Rome, and other places.

The judgment had been made. They had not been silent, as had the citizens of Germany when the smoke from the crematoria had filled their nostrils. This time they had spoken up. They had marshaled many documents of legal evidence to show that the U.S. had broken international law, that the Kellogg-Briand Pact, the Nuremburg Statutes, the Hague Convention, the U.N. Charter all had been violated.

Of course they had. The world is not governed by law, but by power, and the U.S. has the power to break or make any law that is in its interest to do so.

After all, it was the power of the victor that had convened Nuremburg. It is the power of the victor that demands war reparations from the vanquished. It is the small and weak who need law, and law can do no more than request the powerful to respect the rights of the small and weak. Law is successful, of course, only when it is respected by the powerful. The weak are in no position to break it, even if it were in their interest to do so.

Thus, law is a fiction and will remain so until Justice

takes off her blindfold, puts down the scales, and picks up a machine gun.

But the Tribunal chose to use as its foundation the law, and it announced that the U.S. was guilty of "war crimes." It "proved" that it is a "war crime" to bomb little children, peasants, old ladies, hospitals, dikes, churches, etc. It may be a "war crime"; if so, what is a "war legality"? Children above 16 are O.K.? Women under 65? If war itself is not condemned as being criminal, then any weapon used against the "enemy" has to be considered legitimate. There is no nation that goes into battle with copies of the Hague Convention in each soldier's knapsack.

The only "war crime" a soldier knows is not coming back alive.

The legalisms mean nothing. Either one takes a pacifist position and condemns war, or you choose sides. The Tribunal avoided both and simply said, there are certain things which the law says you can't do in a war. This was very reminiscent of what a New York businessman told an Abolitionist, the Rev. Samuel May, in the spring of 1845, when the good cleric had come to the businessman with moral arguments against slavery.

"Mr. May," the businessman told him, "we are not such fools as not to know that slavery is a great evil and a great wrong . . . A great portion of the property of the Southerners is invested under its sanction; and the business of the North, as well as of the South, has become adjusted to it . . . We cannot afford, sir, to let you and your associates succeed in your endeavor to overthrow slavery. It is not a matter of principle with us. It is a matter of business necessity. We cannot afford to let you succeed . . . We do not mean to allow you to succeed. We mean, sir, to put you Abolitionists down—by fair means, if we can, by foul means, if we must."

Lyndon Johnson, lacking the nobility of expression that prevailed in the 19th century, simply laid it on the line when he spoke to U.S. troops at Camp Stanley in Korea in November, 1966: "There are 2 billion of them and 200 million of us. They want what we've got and we're not going to let them get it."

This is the political reality. America is fighting for its own salvation, and you can publish a million photographs of napalmed babies and by the time you've finished, you'll have a million more to publish.

The Tribunal seemed unwilling or unable to deal with the realities of the 1960's. Instead, the members were concerned with making their statements, to let the world know that they were clean. They were not concerned that their acts of conscience be politically effective.

Since World War II, a mystique has grown up around "acts of conscience," as if it were enough, in and of itself, to speak out in the face of injustice. Undoubtedly, it is better to speak than not to speak, but the result of either is too often the same—the political realities remain unchanged.

The War Crimes Tribunal was an act of conscience by European radicals seeking to affect public opinion in the West. It is difficult to believe that these radicals were serious about their task. Every attempt to broaden the scope and approach of the Tribunal was thwarted. In many instances the Tribunal split neatly into two categories—the Europeans vs. the rest. This was particularly apparent on the two occasions when racism in relation to the war was brought up.

The first was after the testimony of a Japanese lawyer who stated that the U.S. would not drop steel-pellet bombs and napalm on Europe, that it was on the Japanese that the atomic bombs had been dropped and that the U.S. was using the Vietnamese to test new weapons. The witness reiterated what he said upon questioning by Courtland Cox.

After the questioning, Gunther Anders said, "I hope you are not trying to say that a war waged by white people against colored people is worse than a war waged by whites against whites. You forget that war was waged in Europe by white people against white people."

The Japanese lawyer made no reply, for what could be said? If one is trying to understand the nature of a war, then one must consider if there are any elements that differ in a war waged by whites against coloreds as opposed to a war waged by whites against whites. Too, one didn't want to embarrass Anders and remind him of the dominant element of World War II—the murder of six million Jews.

Yet the same scene was repeated the following day when Tariq Ali of India testified to the racist character of the war. Upon questioning by Cox, once again, Ali told the following story: "One evening I was standing at the bar of the Hotel Reunification in Hanoi with all of the Canadian members of the International Control Commission who are stationed in Hanoi. One of them said to me, 'I hope the Americans knock the hell out of all these little yellow bastards.' He said it in the hearing of all the Canadians there, and not one of them opened his mouth to disagree."

This time it was Isaac Deutscher who said in patronizing tones, "I trust, gentlemen, that we will not inject race into the discussion." And he continued into various clichés about race not being that important, etc.

Yet the fact remains that at the present time the world is polarizing into West (white) versus everybody else (colored, black, and yellow) and that the war in Vietnam is only a rehearsal for what the U.S. must do if it is to protect its interests in Latin America, other parts of Asia, Africa, and at home. The Tribunal insisted on viewing the war in Vietnam in a vacuum without attempting to relate it to what is happening internationally.

From reading the writings of Sartre one might have expected him to speak out when Deutscher and Anders made their comments on racism and the war. Yet Sartre, along with the other Tribunal members, remained silent.

In many respects the Europeans, particularly the French, dominated and ran the Tribunal. On the very first day, the Japanese, Filipino, and Pakistani members were packing their bags to leave, and some hard persuading had to be done to convince them to stay. Yet the Tribunal never made itself relevant to them or to the Americans.

The Tribunal addressed itself to the U.S. government, the press, and Europe, which is about the same as if Stokely called a press conference on Black Power and invited only the Klan press and expected it to explain Black Power to the black community.

The Tribunal should have addressed itself to the peace movement and the students. The Americans on the Tribunal represented the three organizations that have done the most in opposing the Tribunal—Dellinger of the Spring Mobilization Committee, Oglesby of Students for a Democratic Society, and Cox of the Student Nonviolent Coordinating Committee. When this was mentioned, Sartre's reply was, "America is not the center of the world."

No, it isn't. It *is* the world.

It even controls 75 per cent of France's industry, the major factor behind France's current anti-American stance. America is the country waging the war, and the Tribunal should have addressed itself more to that element in the country opposing the war. Instead, it acted as if the war were going to be stopped on Boulevard Saint Germain-des-Pres.

Perhaps the split in the Tribunal was most obvious on the personal level. It was the Japanese who presented small gifts to the Swedish youth who did all the "dirty work" at the Tribunal—running the mimeograph machine, telephoning, hunting for paper clips, etc. It was the Cubans who presented everyone with a cigar. It was Mr. Kasuri from Pakistan who made a habit of "stealing" the pocketbooks of the girls so that he could sneak bars of candy inside. It was the Americans who found the time to sit down and talk to the Swedish youth and to speak before their student organizations. It was the Europeans who stayed among themselves, energetically maintaining an air of unapproachability.

It is a little thing, perhaps, but there was a noticeable difference between the two groups. You felt that the one group cared about people. I was never sure what the Europeans cared about. Perhaps it was nothing more than their own intellectual commitment.

This was best exemplified near the end of the Tribunal when a debate ensued as to when the Tribunal should render its decision. Some were for waiting two weeks. This would be a good tactic, it was felt, as it would surprise the Tribunal's critics and would serve to create suspense. Others felt that the decision should come immediately. One European said, "The Vietnamese are waiting for our decision." The debate went on until Sartre spoke. "Unless the decision is given immediately I will resign from the Tribunal and issue my own statement."

That settled the issue. It was typical of the kind of blackmail Sartre had practiced throughout the session. Whenever things didn't go his way, he would threaten to resign and issue his own statement. Possibly, he should've been allowed to.

Aside from the information that the Tribunal has amassed and published, it was probably more of a danger than an asset. In an age of revolution, an "act of conscience" is a luxury that cannot be afforded. As Fidel Castro has said, "The job of a revolutionary is to make revolution." The effect of the Tribunal was not toward revolution. Even if it had been toward disruption it would have been more valuable. But it refused to deal with the question of racism; it refused to place U.S. aggression in Vietnam in an international context.

Thus, the nature of the war has only been dimly illuminated and the war itself remains unchallenged. Instead, we have more napalmed babies to contemplate and more atrocities to shock our moral consciences, while David Rockefeller opens a branch of Chase Manhattan in Saigon and the U.S. builds an American-style suburb for 50,000 servicemen outside Saigon and expressways to lead into that city and Danang.

In and of itself, there is nothing wrong with a war crimes tribunal. But the manner in which the session at Stockholm was run amounts to an abdication of responsibility if one's aim is to be politically effective. If the only aim of the Tribunal was to salve the consciences of a few European radicals, I'm certain that they are sleeping well these nights, though the bombs still fall.

The Tribunal was reminiscent of the early days of the civil rights movement when its thrust and motion were toward the moral conscience of America. Nonviolence was the weapon and, it was felt, America could not help but respond positively to the just cause of the movement.

Well, it didn't take long to find out that America has no moral conscience. Every tree that grows in this country was watered by the blood of Indians and Negroes. Recognizing this, the movement has undergone a transformation.

If a man has no moral conscience, threaten his life. So it takes a four-day rebellion in the ghetto to get sprinklers put on the fire hydrants for the summer. You have some idea then what it is going to take to get the U.S. out of Vietnam.

The Tribunal did not recognize this reality and, sadly, showed no interest in even trying to recognize it. Commitment is something that Sartre has written extensively on, and I presume that his involvement at Stockholm was an example of this commitment. If so, possibly what this age needs is not commitment but just caring about other people and being willing to die because you care so much. I couldn't help but feel that Sartre was as much my enemy as LBJ.

Both are men of commitment.

On the last day of the Tribunal I was talking with a Swedish student when a Cambodian who had testified earlier came over to us. He took our hands in his and said in very halting English, "We must not forget that we three, we are comrades." He squeezed our hands tightly, smiling broadly, said a few more words that I didn't catch and waved good-by.

Lord Russell himself may have known something of the

split that existed within the Tribunal, for it was in his closing address, read by Ralph Schoenman, that the real judgment at Stockholm was given:

"The starving and the suffering will no longer die in silence. The Tribunal must inspire a new understanding that the heroic are the oppressed and the hateful are the arrogant rulers who would bleed them for generations or bomb them into the Stone Age. The Tribunal must warn of the impending horror in many lands, the new atrocities prepared now in Vietnam and of the global struggle between the poor and the powerful rich.

"Wherever men struggle against suffering, we must be their voice. Whenever they are cruelly attacked for their self-sacrifice we must find our voices. It is easy to pay lip service to these ideals. *We will be judged not by our reputations or our pretenses but by our will to act.*"

Then, with a dramatic pause, Schoenman turned directly to the members of the Tribunal and, with pronounced deliberation, said: "And we must not forget that those who now sit in judgment will one day be judged by better men."

PUBLISHED IN *The Realist*, MARCH, 1968, as "Final Solutions to the Vietnamese Question."

## THE DUTY OF A REVOLUTIONARY IS . . .

THE duty of a revolutionary is to make the revolution.

That is true, but there are two ambiguous words in the sentence—revolution and revolutionary.

What is a revolutionary?

A revolutionary is one who makes revolution.

But if that is his duty, can he be defined by it? A corporal in the army is more than a corporal in the army. He can be a husband, father, lover, good guy, and a cold-blooded killer. A man is more than the sum of his functions.

Therefore, while it is the revolutionary's duty to make revolution, a revolutionary is more than one who makes revolution.

Before one can make revolution, one must have been revolutionized. The most human people in America are those who have seen the poison in this country and have set themselves against it. Blacks who yell, "Honky!" are revolutionizing themselves. Whites who yell, "LBJ! LBJ! How many kids did you kill today?" are revolutionizing themselves. (Whether these acts will climax in the creation of revolutionaries remains to be seen.)

We must not think of revolution as fighting at the barricades, as hundreds of thousands marching down the streets waving huge flags, as going to the hills with a small band of armed guerrillas, as hiding arms under the floorboards of our bedrooms, as Che Guevara's cigar, as so many romantic images, which aren't romantic when you have to live them. They're difficult and dangerous, and people die in revolutions, like those one million Algerians who died in the war against the French, like the Vietnamese for the past twenty years, like the 45 on the streets of Detroit.

But risking of life,
this dying,
is not the revolution.

It is the natural result of the revolution that takes place inside people when they stand up and shout "NO!" when they stand up and say "ENOUGH!"

Revolution is the ultimate cry of humanity that
humanizes those who before were dehumanized.

It is the ultimate cry of humanity which cannot be bought off, killed or talked out of existence by the *New York Times*.

We are at the minuscule beginning of a revolution. We have seen that everything is upside down in this country and we want to set things right.

And revolution is a turning over, in the same way as the soil is broken and turned over before planting.

It is the ultimate cry of humanity when
it knows that life is more than
working for wages
to buy food,

to buy clothes,
to buy shelter for a day, a week, a
month or a lifetime.
Revolution is when we know
in our very
gut
that food, clothing and shelter are our
rights because we were born.
They are our right because we exist
and that Life is not the procuring
of the necessities,
but the urge toward fulfillment when the
necessities are assured.
One becomes a revolutionary when he
makes a pact with himself, and, then,
with others,
to do whatever is necessary to turn
over the soil and plant new seeds.
It may be necessary to kill so that the
soil may be turned over.
It may be necessary to die so that the
soil may be turned over.
It may be necessary to give up
wife, husband, children, comfort,
everything,
because to make revolution demands
all
of the one who has been revolutionized.
And to be
revolutionized
is to
care so much, so intensely, so deeply,

that every second
of every day is
filled with the pain of seeing what is
and the pain of knowing
what isn't.
Therefore, to be a revolutionary is to
care so much
that one is willing
to die doing his revolutionary duty—
making the revolution.

PUBLISHED IN *The Movement*, DECEMBER, 1967

# PART TWO

# SNCC AND THE ISRAELI-ARAB WAR

THE emotional reactions to the Student Nonviolent Coordinating Committee's recent statements condemning Israel and Zionism have been more interesting than SNCC's own pronouncements. Major Jewish organizations have called SNCC anti-Semitic. One even went so far as to accuse the organization of receiving Arab funds, and this only a few weeks after SNCC had been accused of receiving Cuban money. Theo Bikel and Harry Golden lost their minds and did the impossible—resigned from an organization (SNCC) to which they had never belonged. (The analogous situation would be if Rap Brown called a press conference and announced his resignation as President of the U.S.) Then, out in Chicago at that "happening" on the left, the New Politics convention, blacks showed up and started saying things like "The oppressed have to take the lead in overthrowing oppression" and having caucuses and cussing out white folks. And if that wasn't enough, they went and drew up thirteen resolutions, but many folks never got beyond number five. That was the one that condemned Israel. The resolution explicitly stated that its intent was anti-imperialist and anti-Zionist, not anti-Semitic. It seemed, however, that most read only that Israel was being condemned and followed the path of temporary mindlessness that Bikel and Golden had already gone down.

These reactions are symptomatic of a state of mind that gives the lie to the political pretensions a good number of Jews profess. It is easy to be against the war in Vietnam. In fact, it's the "thing," and, in reality, is little measure of one's political commitment. It is easy to be morally committed, but this should not be confused with political commitment. If one is going to be a radical, he can't go around "flipping out," no matter how emotionally close a particular issue may be to him. On the contrary, it is the radical's responsibility to ask hard, cold questions and not be afraid of the answers.

It is tragic that these questions have not been forthcoming from liberal and radical Jews. Once again it was left to SNCC to act as the gadfly, the prod, pushing and forcing whites deeper into a confrontation with political realities. SNCC has been the spur to the peace movement, refusing to get caught up in intellectual discussions but proclaiming "Hell, no! We won't go!" SNCC had to proclaim Black Power and expel whites from the organization before whites would seriously think about organizing in their communities. Once again the organization refused to play it safe and keep what little nonblack support it still had. It condemned Israel and Zionism, expecting the reaction that came, but hoping that some discussion and dialogue would be started within the Jewish-liberal-radical camp about Israel's role in the Middle East and Africa. Instead, the most blatant lack of political integrity has been justified by the cry of "anti-Semitism."

This reaction only points up that Jews are still Hitler's victims, both here and in Israel. Israel's existence and any of its subsequent acts are supposedly justified because of the six million who were murdered in the gas chambers. And to say the contrary is to be anti-Semitic and to spit on the graves of those six million. Because these were murdered, Jews have built a vast reservoir of sympathy on which they trade liberally. Israel's support in the Western mind is based on this guilt, this pity. Israel's militarism is designed to erase that nagging image of the meek Jew going to take a "shower," and most American Jews never felt more pride than they did at Israel's military victory over the Arabs. It is obvious that the Jews wish to feel vindicated, but it was not the Arabs who oppressed them.

It is the responsibility of the politically concerned person to be honest. He will be ineffective if he is not. Any Jew who does not question Israel's very existence nullifies any meaning his opposition to the war in Vietnam may have. And to accuse those who do raise questions of being anti-Semitic is to brand yourself as a potential enemy.

It is interesting to note that Germany is producing a generation of writers who are painfully examining the Hitler era and their own involvement in it. Such has not as yet happened among Jews. The ghosts of those six million yet haunt us. They must never be forgotten, but they must be laid to rest. The political realities of this age demand it.

October 14, 1967

## CONFRONTATION AT THE PENTAGON

THEY had come for a confrontation at the Pentagon and their mood was almost carnival-like until they saw it. Many wore cards reading, "We don't want violence," but they felt ridiculous when they stood in front of the international headquarters of violence. The Pentagon is an impressive structure, a five-sided fortress, but those granite walls didn't awe anyone. It made them angry. It made them so angry that the confrontation began sooner than had been planned and it developed into more than had been expected.

For over an hour after they arrived at the Pentagon, thousands of demonstrators stood toe to toe with the Military Police and federal marshals. It was obvious that this stand-off was as far as things were to proceed. The MP's would not treat the demonstrators like a bunch of niggers and wade in with billy clubs and tear gas to disperse the crowd. They would allow them to make their protest and then go home, with only a few zealous ones arrested, a few militants bleeding.

It might have worked, because no one was anxious to get his head broken or to be speared by a bayonet. It might have worked, but people were not there to be stalemated. Eventually one contingent of MP's decided to take control of the area just below the steps on the north side of the mall. With rifles pointed, they charged toward the demonstrators, and it was here that the demonstrators showed that they had moved beyond protest. When the MP's pushed, the demonstrators pushed back. Instead of backing up at the sight of rifles pointed at them, they surrounded the MP's, and several demonstrators used the poles to which their picket signs were attached to get in a few hard licks. One MP was jerked out of line, shoved into a corner, and set upon by demonstrators. He was rescued, but there was one demonstrator who proudly wore an MP's helmet for the rest of the day.

Eventually the MP's realized that they were merely provoking the crowd and retreated. Also, they had been humiliated. How would you feel if you pointed a rifle at someone, put on your grimmest expression, and then had somebody stick a flower into the barrel? How would you feel standing shoulder to shoulder with your fellow Army comrades to be suddenly deluged by a shower of flowers and end up with flowers hanging from the brim of your helmet?

The confrontation finally came on the south side of the mall, where demonstrators massed in the driveway leading to the door of the Pentagon and broke through the line of MP's and marshals, charging toward the front door of the Pentagon. They were repulsed, but time and time again they broke through the lines, up the driveway and toward the front door. Eventually the Army relinquished control of a good portion of the driveway and retreated to maintain control of the front door.

It was obvious that this was a new peace movement. Many a marshal swung his billy club, and instead of it crashing into a nonresistant skull, the club was torn from the marshal's hands. Many a soldier who pointed his rifle at a crowd was laughed at. It is crucial, however, that the peace movement not become too elated with its success. The victory was only a victory because the Army did not unleash its power. Rifles that could have been fired into the air (or in a more horizontal direction) remained silent. Clubs that could have been wielded with the viciousness that blacks know, were used sparingly. Some tear gas was used, but not on the scale that it could have been. Lyndon Johnson refused to do to the thousands of whites what has been done countless times to blacks. If he had done so, there would have been no confrontation. The Army could have cleared the Pentagon mall in a matter of minutes. The next time or the time after that, they will, and if the demonstrators are as well-prepared as they were this time, they will be massacred. A flower is a good weapon only when the guns are not fired. A body is a good weapon only when the billy clubs are not swung with automated efficiency and tear gas used as if it were a squirt of nasal spray for head colds. It was a victory only because the powerful did not use their power.

It must be remembered that the demonstrators were to some degree immune from wholesale brutality because they were white and because they were middle-class. Whether they retain their racial and class immunity depends on their militancy and degree of developed action. If they become a real threat to this country, they will lose that immunity.

The confrontation at the Pentagon shows graphically for the first time that the revolutionary potential of young whites is no longer simply a matter of conjecture.

If that potential is to become a reality, it must be learned that it is not only the war in Vietnam that must be stopped. It is this country. One demonstrator cried out during a brief skirmish between demonstrators and the Army: "Humanity is dead in America!" In the broadest terms that is the issue. But humanity is not synonymous with flowers in the hair and bells on the feet. Neither is it synonymous with slogans on a picket sign or marching on the Pentagon. Whether a country is humane is directly related to the economic and political system under which that country's citizens live. It is not enough to be against the war in Vietnam, because next year one might have to be against the war in Bolivia, but it will be the same war. A war is a war when that war is fought to sustain the present political and economic system. The place name is only incidental.

It is good that people are now so angry that they will storm the Pentagon. The next step is to let the anger come not only from what is being done to the Vietnamese, but to all the people of Africa, Asia, Latin America, and to blacks here. And above all, it must be realized that this government's very existence is a constant act of war against every one of us.

OCTOBER 28, 1967

## THE LEGALISMS OF REPRESSION

THE myths of freedom that exist in this country have lulled us into thinking that we can preach revolution under the constitutional provisions of free speech and thereby escape the consequences of that preaching. That is true only as long as the preaching does not constitute a threat to the system. America loves a part of the preaching because it indicates the weaknesses that need to be eradicated if the system is to preserve itself. However, once that preaching shifts from an attack upon a particular act of the government to an attack against the system upon which the government is built, the government will, of course, retaliate.

Because of the romance that attaches itself to the idea of revolution in this country, we have been led to believe that that retaliation will take the most violent and brutal forms. That is the political error the government wants us to make. It wants us to become paranoics, waiting for the squads of policemen to break down the doors and throw people into prisons and concentration camps. It is true that some organizations have been subjected to incidents of this kind, but these organizations could be so treated because they did not have mass support and there would be no mass protest over their being persecuted. Other organizations, such as Students for a Democratic Society and the Student Nonviolent Coordinating Committee, enjoy a degree of immunity from this kind of persecution because there would be mass demonstrations stemming from any attempt to brutally suppress them. Thus, the government has to move in a much more "legal" way. It will attempt to isolate the more organized groups who have popular support from liberals; it will attempt to increase the isolation between black and white. Once each dangerous element has been isolated, it can be eliminated, one by one.

In a democratic society, democratic means are used to suppress. The SS troops are used only when the democratic means have failed. And the government has not begun in earnest to use its democratic machinery against us. It has begun, however, and the left, black and white, is going to find its revolutionary ideals and rhetoric tested. Revolutionaries are not made in libraries; their reality depends upon their response to suppression and persecution.

It should have been apparent what was happening when H. Rap Brown was arrested for carrying a gun across state lines while under federal indictment. It is a "jive" charge, as the brothers on the block would say, but growing out of it was a court order restricting Brown's movements to the Southern District of New York. That done, the government rested its case, because it had accomplished its purpose. H. Rap Brown was no longer free to travel around the country and speak. He was a political prisoner, and his jail would be Manhattan Island. Of course, he has the constitutional right of free speech, but we're fools if we think the government is going to consider the constitutional rights of a man telling people the country should be burned down.

From there it is a quiet step to the next move, which the government began two weeks ago. The Senate Internal Security Subcommittee announced that it was opening hearings on the New Left. At the same time, the House Un-American Activities Committee opened hearings on the rebellions of this past summer. Also, at the same time, the Senate Permanent Investigations Subcommittee opened hearings on the rebellions. And, at the same time once again, the Senate passed the Dirksen bill, which will allow the Subversive Activities Control Board to cite anyone it wishes as communist and list his name with the Attorney General, who will make the list public.

Thus, the stage is set and the curtain raised. We should not have to wait to see the play, because we are the principal actors and the script is an old one. Senator Joe McCarthy was the most recent director and producer of this play, but we will make a mistake if we expect another McCarthy. The play's director will not come from the right, but from the center—the liberals.

The new director will be someone like Daniel P. Moynihan of Moynihan Report fame, now director of the Harvard-MIT Center for Urban Studies and member of Bobby Kennedy's brain trust. James Reston in the *New York Times* characterized him as one who sees "that the rise in violence is nothing less than a fundamental challenge against the present foreign policy and social order of the United States." He believes that "the violence at home and abroad has the potential for polarizing, then fracturing American society. He believes it threatens the social order in the country and that liberals . . . must make a new alliance with progressive conservatives to deal with the extremists of right and left and give the states and cities much more responsibility and resources for dealing with the home front." He calls such a coalition of liberals and conservatives "the politics of stability." It is more commonly known as fascism.

Thus, the government has begun to move, and it will move rapidly between now and the '68 elections to control dissent here and to end the war in Vietnam. It does not realize that many who talk revolution may be doing so because it sounds good; it cannot afford to take any chances that this is talk of young minds and loose tongues. So it begins to move quietly to deal with the dissidents. So quietly and so skillfully will it move that the left will have disappeared for two weeks before anyone realizes what has happened.

This will be true, unless we understand what is happening and act before it acts and not in reaction to its actions. We have a choice. We can prepare ourselves for an ordeal and suffer with nobility. Or we can test ourselves as revolutionaries, organize our ranks, mobilize people, and go forward to do battle.

We are not engaged in a game of badminton in a park. The government realizes this more than we do at this point. Neither this country nor this world is big enough for revolutionary and reactionary forces. One has to be eliminated. The government's determination that we are the ones to be eliminated, by any means necessary, should never be underestimated. Particularly now.

November 11, 1967

## CHE GUEVARA AND THE CULT OF THE PERSONALITY

SINCE the death of Che, much of the left press has printed articles on his life and thought. Most of these tributes have damned the "international thugs of imperialism" for his death and praised Che's "heroic revolutionary spirit." There have also been memorial meetings for Che which have generally been a monotonous continuum of speeches on the order of "Now, the first time I met Che . . . And the next time I saw Che was . . ." These were interspersed with the What-a-Great-Revolutionary-Che-Was speech.

The articles and meetings are understandable, even if the audience has been left with very little in the end. More disturbing has been the appearance of the vultures of the left with their buttons ("Avenge Che") and posters bearing his image. It is all too reminiscent of and no different from the vultures who descended to exploit the death of John Kennedy. One expects no less from those whose object is to make a profit from death, destruction, fire, or flood. One expects more from those who consider themselves, and wish to be considered, revolutionaries.

In the articles, meetings, posters, and buttons that have

appeared since the death of Che, the emphasis of each has been upon Che the man. Speakers have speeched and writers have written upon his fine qualities until he has begun to obtain mythical proportions. This emphasis upon Che as an individual is a reflection of the individualistic orientation of much of the left and a reflection of how American, rather than political, the left can be sometimes.

We are taught history in school as if it were a succession of great men. These great men are held up to us as models we should emulate. Don't lie because George Washington didn't. Like niggers because Abraham Lincoln did. Help the poor because Franklin D. Roosevelt did. Having been given heroes since childhood, it is logical that upon assuming adulthood the need for heroes and models is still evident. But we are too sophisticated at that point to continue to believe in Washington, Lincoln and Roosevelt. Thus, when a Stokely Carmichael, Rap Brown, Fidel Castro, Mao Tse-tung, and Che Guevara come into our consciousness, they fill the vacuum created by the demise of our school heroes. We admire one who is considered revolutionary and by a process of perverse logic come to the conclusion that we, too, are revolutionary.

The emphasis upon Che the man obscures the fact that Che was who he was because he was involved in the revolutionary process, just as Lyndon Johnson is who he is because of his involvement in the counterrevolutionary process. To separate Che from the revolutionary process is to do a disservice to him as well as a disservice to ourselves.

It is not wrong to want to emulate Che. It is not wrong to have a poster of his image on one's wall. But it is the responsibility of those who are now pushing the image of Che to put him in the context of the revolutionary process and not in the context of myth. The impact of the revolutionary experience (the experience that changes man) can be seen not only in the person of Che Guevara, but also in the person of each Cuban citizen, in the person of each citizen of North Vietnam.

Che is extraordinary to most minds on the left because that kind of individual is hardly known in this country. Those who do exist here have become that way because of their involvement in the revolutionary process, i.e., they have been revolutionized.

Those who give us posters of Che's image to put on our walls and buttons to wear on our chests impede understanding of the revolutionary process because they point us away from our responsibility to ourselves. That responsibility is not to be like Che. That responsibility is to do what Che did —become a part of the revolutionary experience and find fulfillment. Thereby will the 21st-century man that Che wrote of be created.

Heroes are necessary only in a society where man is unfulfilled and has to seek that fulfillment through the vicarious experience of identifying with heroes. It does not speak well of those who proclaim revolutionary allegiance to be involved in hero worship. It is not Che as a hero whom we need. Rather it is to understand how a Che Guevara was molded. That understanding, however, can come only from involvement. It is, perhaps, that which the hero worshipers and vultures lack.

November 25, 1967

# THE NECESSITY OF VIOLENCE

VIOLENCE is neither good nor evil. It is. So if we are going to fight to humanize America, i.e., make revolution, let us not concern ourselves with moral arguments over the legitimacy of violence. It exists and we acknowledge the fact.

Violence is used as an instrument against us when we demonstrate against recruiters from Dow Chemical, the Pentagon, Dean Rusk, President Johnson. Violence is used as an instrument against blacks in the course of their day-to-day lives. Violence is used against the Vietnamese in the course of their day-to-day lives. They are communists, we are told. You will never make me believe that a man deserves to die because of his political beliefs. In reality, no man deserves to die, be injured, maimed, or brutalized in any way. Yet we are killed, injured, maimed, and brutalized every day. We recognize that we do not deserve it. Yet it is done to us. We are told that we exist to serve our country. I would think that we exist first to be served by our country and give our service in return, because we are the country. The government resides in and with us; we are not the instruments of a government.

When we put ourselves in opposition to the violence perpetrated against us, we cannot beg, plead, petition, or request the perpetrators of violence to desist. Their violence will only accelerate itself. We must recognize that they have no right to be violent against us. It is our responsibility to stop them. No man deserves to die at the hand of another except he who refuses to lay down his arms when asked. Once he refuses, he must be forced. If a man tries to take my life, he is, in effect, giving me permission to try and take his life. The Ku Klux Klan has never had any difficulty realizing this. They thought blacks threatened their lives and used violence as a means to maintain them. The Minutemen see a communist conspiracy and are armed to defend the lives they love. We know that blacks are not a threat to poor white Southerners; we know that there is no communist conspiracy. But that is not the point. The Klan and the Minutemen have never equivocated about the use of violence to defend their beliefs. We know that the government of this country has never argued over whether violence should be used against anybody in the world. The argument is simply over how much.

Why, then, do we debate, argue and equivocate about using violence when our lives are threatened? Why, then, do we feel that our souls will be irreparably polluted by the use of violence?

Violence is not good or evil. It is necessary. Today we have our Nat Turners on the street corners of every ghetto, but where are our John Browns? Where are our men and women so filled with anger and indignation at what this country is doing to them that they will mount their horses and ride through the Lawrence, Kansas, of America, saying, "No more. No more. I want to live."

"Posterity will owe everlasting thanks to John Brown," Frederick Douglass wrote. "He has attacked slavery with the weapons precisely adapted to bring it to death. Moral considerations have long since been exhausted upon slaveholders. It is in vain to reason with them . . . Slavery is a system of brute force. It shields itself behind might, rather than right. It must be met with its own weapons."

America has always shielded itself behind might. We must meet it with its own weapons.

December 9, 1967

# THE WHITE RADICAL AS REVOLUTIONARY

THE white radical has generally been afflicted with overwhelming feelings of guilt in the presence of blacks. While knowing rationally that he has never consciously been an oppressor of blacks, the guilt is there. To pay for his "sins," the white radical has adopted an attitude of sycophancy, which has led to the conclusion that everything black is good, and Oh, woe is me that I wasn't born black. The white radical has come to feel that his actions aren't valid if blacks do not participate in them. In essence, nothing that he does or thinks is valid unless it has been given the black stamp of approval.

This attitude is harmful to the development of a non-black revolutionary cadre. It is true that the black movement at this time is a vital and dynamic one and its energy was the largest single factor in the creation of a young, non-black radical movement. The most obvious is the fact that blacks are the most oppressed; thus, when they began to organize, they had plenty to fight against and plenty to fight for. Their targets were concrete and their enemy was felt daily in their lives.

The nonblack movement started from a different point. What blacks felt in the gut, whites felt in the mind. They knew that certain things were unjust and began to speak out against these injustices. Blacks knew that certain things stifled their lives and began to fight for their survival.

When the sit-in movement began in 1960, northern white students supported it by sending telegrams of encouragement to the black students in the South and by picketing the offices of variety chain stores in the North. In 1961 and 1962 the involvement increased when whites began coming South to work with the Student Nonviolent Coordinating Committee and the Congress of Racial Equality. Parallel with this were the demonstrations in the North against U.S. involvement in Cuba and demonstrations for the nuclear test ban treaty. White involvement in the civil rights movement reached an apex with the Mississippi Summer Project in 1964. After that, white radical attention shifted to Vietnam, where it has remained and grown.

Whites were always peripheral to the civil rights movement while actively involved in it. It served as a valuable training ground for many and an opportunity to test their commitment. The white radical, however, always saw himself in a direct relationship with the black radical and was, therefore, stunned at the enunciation of Black Power and black nationalism. The result was a loss of direction for the white radical.

The black radical movement and the white radical movement have started from different points. By necessity blacks have had to organize around their blackness, because their blackness has been used as an oppressive force against them. Whites, by necessity, cannot organize around whiteness because it is whiteness that has been used as an oppressing force. This is the crux of the matter. White radicals allow themselves to be turned into sycophants because they identify as whites. They feel guilty when a black speaks of whites as racists and honkies because they identify as whites. And in actuality, there is no need for the white radical to identify on a basis of color, and, in particular, to identify as whites.

As it is used by black radicals, the word "white" has been misunderstood. It should be obvious that no man is guilty on the basis of his skin color. He is guilty if he identifies with what that skin color has come to represent to blacks, i.e., racism, oppression, and exploitation. It is this which the words "whitey," "cracker," and "honky" combat. Any white radical who is fighting against oppression, exploitation, and all that "white" represents, should be able to yell "honky" as loud as any black.

Because of the necessity for racial identification in the black movement, it has to be separate from the white movement. This is as it should be at this time and should cause no one to despair. Whites have to learn many things that blacks already know; blacks must learn many things that whites already know. While going their separate ways, white radicals must reach the point where they react to the racism that inevitably exists in them (because they grew up here), not by guilt and sycophancy, but by choosing not to identify with the government but with the oppressed and the dispossessed (which they are, if they would only realize it). Any white who can speak of "my country" is an automatic enemy of blacks because he is choosing to identify himself with oppression, exploitation, and racism. It is "their country"; we're fighting to make it ours.

The only identification that a white radical can have is as a revolutionary committed to the destruction of the present system. Anything less is to identify oneself with that system and its values, and that is to be identified by the color of your skin and to be branded as the enemy. (Go home and call your father a honky and see how liberated you'll feel.)

DECEMBER 23, 1967

## THE HOUSE ARREST OF H. RAP BROWN

IN that other U.S.A., the Union of South Africa, many "lawful" techniques have been developed for controlling dissidents. One of the more well-known is "house arrest," where the home becomes the jail, from which one leaves only at specified hours and to which no one comes.

In this U.S.A., the authorities would never be so crude as to make one a prisoner in his living room. The American moral conscience would not accept this (for a while). Thus, a more subtle form of "house arrest" is being tested now in the travel ban that has been imposed on H. Rap Brown.

Since the last week of September, Brown has been under a court injunction limiting his travel to New York City (Queens and Brooklyn are off limits) and a few counties north of New York City. When he was arrested in July after the rebellion in Cambridge, Md., one of the conditions for his release from jail was this restriction on his travel. This can be called "preventative arrest," i.e., if you think someone is going to be going around the country telling the truth about you, you fix it so he can't. Instead of locking him in jail and throwing away the key, it's much easier to let the person live at home, walk around when and where he wants to, except you don't let him leave the city or the state. Thus, he is stopped from going around the country and putting you up-tight.

Brown is not the first person to be thus incarcerated. During the Harlem rebellion of 1964, Bill Epton of the Progressive Labor Party was arrested for sedition and released on bail on the condition that he would not be allowed to travel out of New York. Shortly thereafter, another PLP member on the West Coast was arrested on the same charge and is now restricted to the state of California. Most recently, Eddie Oquendo, who refused to be drafted because he was opposed to the Vietnam war, has had his movements restricted to the borough of Brooklyn. (To be restricted to Brooklyn is perhaps worse than jail.)

Brown's attorneys appealed the travel restriction against him to Chief Justice Earl Warren (of Warren Commission fame), who refused to do anything. The case has now been appealed to the full Supreme Court. It is apparent that if the government is able to keep Brown under "lock and key," it will be able to move with impunity against lesser-known radicals. It is important, therefore, that pressure be put on the government for the release of H. Rap Brown.

It is not only the rights of H. Rap Brown that are important and are at stake here. It is the rights of each and every one of us. If it can happen to him, a nationally known figure, you damn well better believe it can happen to us who are strangers on the next block. A concentration camp can be made out of blue sky and earth if you aren't free to walk where you wish beneath that sky and upon that earth.

DECEMBER 30, 1967

# RADICALS AND THE MEDIA

ONE of the more blatant lies propounded in America is the one about "freedom of the press." That illusion can be fostered because of the existence of, for example, a *New York Daily News* (conservative) and a *New York Times* (liberal) publishing in the same city every day. This is "freedom of the press" because varying points of views are expressed in the two papers. That is true, but there is a difference of degree, not of kind, because both newspapers operate within the same framework. The differences that exist are superficial, no matter how different the rhetoric.

For example, the *New York Times* is more "liberal" because it is opposed to the bombing of North Vietnam. The *Daily News* is conservative because it wants the bombing escalated. Yet the two newspapers agree that "communism" should be stopped and that the "sovereignty" of South Vietnam should be preserved. Their disagreement comes on how this should be accomplished. (Doves are hawks in sheeps' clothing.)

The American press is not free, because it accepts the ideology of the government and the system. It does not editorialize against capitalism, imperialism, or free enterprise. It does not question the status quo; it merely suggests various means by which the status quo may prevail. Thus, we have, in effect, a government-controlled press, because that press is not opposed to the government, but merely to the way the government does what it does.

Because it is a government-controlled press, its reportage of protest and resistance activities, organizations, etc., reflects this bias. It reports events in such a manner that the reportage becomes a weapon to stifle anti-government activity and a weapon to rally government support. This modus operandi can be called "negative news."

Example: In the early decades of this century, whites attacked and killed blacks on numerous occasions. These were reported as "race riots," though it was the whites who were armed and it was blacks who died. What would have been the effect if they had been reported as "massacres," which in fact they were.

Example: The rebellions of 1967 have been reported as "riots," creating the impression of barbarism and anarchy running rampant in the country. To have reported them as "rebellions" would have been to admit that blacks had a legitimate right to act as they did.

Example: Press coverage of Stokely Carmichael and Rap Brown has made them appear like raving maniacs. And a hysteria among whites has been created thereby. However, the "negative news" coverage of Carmichael and Brown backfired to the extent that it made them leaders and heroes in the black community. Thus, the almost total press blackout on Carmichael and Brown in recent months.

The only relationship the press can have to any radical or revolutionary organization is negative, to be used as tools for the government. It is impossible, of course, for the left to avoid the government-controlled press. However, it is possible for the left to minimize contact with that press, and, to some degree, control the treatment it receives at the hands of that press. But it must be realized that the press and television can in no way be used by the left to communicate with people. It is not the function of the press to report; its function is to shape opinion.

It therefore becomes necessary for the left to develop its own means of communication. These can stem from leaflets to newspapers. The Underground Press is a good development, as are newspapers such as *The Movement,* the *SNCC Newsletter, Muhammad Speaks, The Guardian,* and others.

Yet a newspaper is not the only means of communication. Leaflets have seldom been utilized except to announce meetings and demonstrations. A simple four-fold leaflet, printed back and front, can contain a lot of information. Also, there are not many posters available that communicate political concepts. Posters of Stokely, Che and Mao are okay, but they are mainly for us to put on our walls. Generally we spend too much time talking to ourselves about what we may already know. Talking to each other is necessary. Equally as necessary is talking to those who disagree with us or are uncommitted. An effective poster or handbill passed out in front of grocery stores on weekends is a necessary step that must be utilized widely in the coming months.

Twenty-four hours a day the government-controlled media are shaping opinions and attitudes in this country. We cannot use those media for our ends. If they're working twenty-four hours a day, we must begin working forty-eight hours a day (at a minimum). Our communications network can be more effective than theirs if we begin to understand the immense power that people have when their political ideology is correct and when they know the best way to communicate it.

JANUARY 6, 1968

## AGENTS AND RADICAL ORGANIZATIONS

ONE of the more difficult problems faced by radical organizations is how to guard against and detect agents. Some individuals think that they are dealing with the problem by getting paranoid and seeing plots and agents in the way the sun may be shining through the clouds. One must maintain an attitude of "constant vigilance" and "constant mistrust," as Che Guevara pointed out, but not to the degree that one becomes immobilized. This is what is happening to a good number of people. When vigilance results in immobility, it is a victory for the enemy. He can either immobilize you through subversion or through your own fears. Either way we lose.

It must be realized that there is absolutely no way to guard against agents. A radical organization has to be open enough to accept new recruits, and while it should not welcome with open arms everybody who walks through the door, there has to be an attitude of minimal trust within one's attitude of constant mistrust. To say that everyone black is a "brother" is nice, but don't believe it. It is a difficult fact to live with, but you can never be totally sure about anyone. Lenin's closest associate was an agent of the Czar, a fact not learned until after the revolution. Does this mean that you trust no one? No. It means that a well-organized cadre cannot be subverted by police agents.

The good revolutionary realizes that while the enemy is powerful and well-organized and should never be underestimated, the enemy is, in reality, a paper tiger. His power rests in his weapons and technology; the revolutionary's power rests in the correctness of his ideology and the understanding of the people of that ideology. To many of us it seems ludicrous that the Chinese championship Ping-Pong team should point to the teachings of Chairman Mao as being the reason for their success. Nothing is more logical than that a correct ideology correctly applied cannot be defeated.

We cannot win yet because we do not understand what we are fighting against or what we are fighting for. We become afraid, because we do not understand. We do not talk on the telephone because the line is tapped. Then perhaps we should not talk, because the government has listening devices that can be stationed three blocks from where you are and pick up a quiet belch. This does not mean you broadcast everything you're going to do. It simply means that you must organize in such a way that even if the enemy knows what you're going to do (and he does), he can't defeat it.

One does not guard against agents by playing safe. To play safe is to play the enemy's game. The possibility of winning all is created only when all is risked.

One can guard against agents by knowing whom you

work with and by saying only what is necessary at any given time. There is never any necessity for everyone to know everything. One need know only what is necessary for him to do his job. No more. One should always be suspicious of those who sound most radical. It is all right to talk about killing cops, but this has to be done within a particular framework. What will be gained? What will be the follow-up? While the cop's blood is flowing, how do we make sure our blood does not flow? He who advocates violence without talking about how to prevent needless loss of life is either an agent or politically immature. He who sounds most militant may not be political, only frustrated. This can be easily ascertained if the cadre has the correct theory.

Ultimately, correct ideology is the only way to insure an organization's survival and effectiveness with agents in its midst. It is ideology that we lack at present. Too many are involved because of personal hang-ups and not commitment. The winds of repression are blowing, however, and the wheat and the chaff will be separated. Those who have scorned the necessity for ideology will find themselves full of fear when the enemy forces us to decide which side we are on.

There is perhaps more to fear from the radical romantics and uncommitted than police agents. The former are, in effect, unconscious agents, because the result of their actions is the same as that of the police agents—subversion and disruption. The police agent knows what he is about. The unconscious agent does not, and his ignorance can get a lot of people killed needlessly. Correct ideology is the only weapon for dealing with any agent.

JANUARY 20, 1968

## AGENTS AND DEMONSTRATIONS

THE skilled use of police agents during the week of demonstrations in New York in December pointed up just how far we have to go before we can consider ourselves really organized.

Agents dressed as hippies and students not only were able to create confusion in the crowds of demonstrators, sometimes leading them into police traps to be beaten and arrested, but they also "fingered" demonstration leaders and well-known radicals for uniformed police to give special attention to. One leader "fingered" by an agent was arrested on a disorderly conduct charge while standing in a phone booth making a call.

In a mass demonstration it is impossible not to be infiltrated. It therefore becomes of paramount importance that the demonstrators know what they're about in advance and that the groups involved be in a position to enforce discipline upon the demonstrators.

This is simple for radical pacifists. The discipline is nonviolence, and anyone who begins to deviate from this is generally stopped by the group before the police can intervene. For nonpacifist radicals the problem is much more difficult.

Still pervading radical organizations is the laissez-faire attitude of, "Well, come and do your thing." And the first ones there to "do their thing" are police agents. Also, inviting everyone to come and "do their thing" means that a lot of pacifists come who unintentionally quite often get people arrested and beaten when that could have been avoided. Pacifists at demonstrations that are called by nonpacifists can have the same effect as agents—the demonstration is effectively disrupted. It is perhaps time for radicals to realize a painful truth: There can be no long-term, effective coalition between conflicting ideologies. If your ultimate goal is to blow up an induction center and theirs is to block its doors, there is no common basis for action unless you see blocking the doors as an opportunity to lay the dynamite.

But the nonpacifist radical has developed no tactics of violence as yet. A few are developing among a small minority, but this is only among those who have decided that their commitment is to a revolutionary movement and not only a commitment to get the troops out of Vietnam. It is within this developing cadre that there exists the means for dealing with agents at demonstrations. A political cadre has first and above all else an ideology, a definite position, which enables it to respond immediately to any situation. A member of a political cadre becomes an Othello, who in Hamlet's situation would have done away with the king before taking his coat off, instead of agonizing for five acts and ending up dead himself. Right now there are all too many Hamlets who insist on examining the issue from all sides, taking into account everybody's point of view and not wanting to offend anyone, not even the police.

Thus, when demonstrators stand facing the police and someone yells, "Let's get the cops!," the organized cadre can immediately move in and get that guy out of the crowd or shut him up, because unless people are carrying baseball bats in addition to wearing helmets, it's obvious that the guy yelling is either an agent or just plain dumb. The cadre can also organize a predemonstration demonstration for practice, to decide how to counter every move the cops make and to give the people a way to analyze what is happening. The success of demonstrations now depends upon how many hours are spent beforehand with maps, anticipating what the cops will do and learning how to get in and out of any area by streets and by rooftops. And, of course all information concerning the demonstration cannot be given in advance. The cadre must have the faith of the people. It is the primary work of the cadre to win that faith and the primary responsibility of the cadre to maintain and be worthy of that faith.

The December demonstrations in New York can be considered a failure only if nothing has been learned. They indicated that the success at the Pentagon was a lot of luck. That luck didn't hold at Whitehall Street. Luck has never won a revolution. Organization, ideology, and work win revolutions. And if one needs a good example, look at Vince Lombardi and the Green Bay Packers. Where, pray tell, is the Vince Lombardi of the left?

JANUARY 27, 1968

## THE OPPRESSION OF WHITES

THE potential for revolution in this country will remain unrealized until whites understand that they are an oppressed people. Oppression is generally thought of as a condition endured only by blacks, Puerto Ricans, Mexican-Americans, and the poor whites of the South. Oppression is associated with the poverty of Appalachia and the tenements of Harlem, but a rundown mountain shack and a rat-infested tenement are only an aspect of oppression—material deprivation.

Oppression is a condition common to all of us who are without the power to make the decisions that govern the political, economic, and social life of this country. We are oppressed because our lives are predetermined by an economic and political philosophy that is based upon oppression. We are educated to fit into the economic structure of the nation, to perform our allotted tasks to keep that economic machine functioning, and eventually to die, having lived our lives "earning a living." We are oppressed because to "earn a living" (work), we are told, is good; to refuse to "earn a living," voluntarily or involuntarily, is bad. Two weeks of every fifty-two are allotted to us to live. The other fifty are spent being "good," i.e., keeping the economic machine functioning. Our reward for being "good" is a salary, a pacifier with which we feed, clothe, and house ourselves and our families and dull the pain by going into debt to buy the luxury items which give us the illusion of life.

It is necessary for the white radical to analyze the nature of his oppression and realize that any person who earns wages is a member of the working class. The taxi driver and the college professor are equal members of the working class. The professor's salary and social status give him certain attitudes whereby he can believe himself to be different. He is middle-class, bourgeois, but he is still a part of the working class. The middle class and the working class are not opposed to each other. The middle class is only a particular classification within the working class, and in the American context, working class must be defined anew. Middle class must be defined anew.

Whites are oppressed, but their realization of this is as yet, for the most part, unconscious. The hippie phenomenon, the widespread use of drugs, the teen-age runaways and the anti-war movement are all reactions to oppression. But the nature and substance of that oppression is only faintly articulated. Until a people understand what is being done to them, they will react only to what is hostile to their well-being. They will not fight against it.

Perhaps the basic inability of black radicals and whites to communicate lies in the fact that the former know acutely the nature of oppression, while whites still think they're free. They still find it difficult not to believe the fairy tales about this country taught in school. Blacks know what has been done to them and they are angry. Whites do not and thus can only romantically identify with the anger of blacks.

Yet we are all victims of the ideology of inhumanity on which this country thrives. It is an ideology which says that if the amount of money in a man's pocket does not correspond to some numbers on a tag, that man can starve, be kicked out of his home, and go naked. It is an ideology of death, whose most blatant manifestation is napalm. But napalm is the logical extension of an ideology which requires money in exchange for the basic necessities of life.

There is much talk and confusion as to how to organize whites. Few feel adequate to the task and rationalize by saying that it is much easier to organize in the black community. Yet, all around us there are whites who are trying to get out of the system the best way they can. For most it is no more than sitting in front of the television set with a can of beer night after night and being anesthetized. Whites use a myriad of drugs to dull the pain. They do not want their perception of reality heightened. It is heightened too much already, and if they can't dull the pain, they eventually go quietly berserk one day. How many times a week do we read of some quiet model citizen eliminating his wife, kids, and himself and leaving no explanation behind for the neighbors. The neighbors don't need it explained, however. They know.

The inhumanity of America is etched into the lines of every white face. Yet the white radical tends to look upon whites with contempt. But talk to a cab driver, a waitress, one of those chic young secretaries, an airline stewardess, and the pain and misery they live is immediately apparent. Just as the absence of physical comfort reflects the oppression of the Kentucky miner, the absence of any semblance of a whole man reflects the oppression of those who have physical comfort.

The phrase that is being used to characterize the antiwar movement now is "from protest to resistance." That's true on one level, but the real battle has not yet been joined. That is the struggle against oppression. All that is evident now are the reactions to oppression. It is the responsibility of the white radical to move from reaction to oppression to action against it.

FEBRUARY 3, 1968

# THE ORANGEBURG MASSACRE

FOR THOSE WHITES who have had difficulty comprehending the violent mood pervading the black community, perhaps the Orangeburg (South Carolina) Massacre of February 8 will make understanding a little less difficult. In the eight-year history of the black movement, there have been many instances of violence perpetrated by whites against blacks, but none so impossible to take as Orangeburg.

Orangeburg itself was one of the early battlegrounds of the civil rights movement. In the winter of 1961, Student Nonviolent Coordinating Committee organizers helped lead demonstrations against segregated public facilities there. Hundreds were arrested and herded into a stockade, where they were hosed for several hours by the fire department. Since that time, white man's progress has come to Orangeburg, and in response to a demonstration against a segregated bowling alley, the police, state troopers and National Guard murdered three black students and injured fifty others. Among those injured, arrested, and held on $50,000 bail in the South Carolina State Penitentiary was the former SNCC program director, Cleve Sellers.

The Orangeburg Massacre comes after eight years of beatings, jailings, and murders of blacks by whites in the course of the black liberation movement. There were thirteen blacks killed during the Mississippi Summer Project of 1964, the four young girls killed in the church bombing in Birmingham, Jimmy Lee Jackson and the hundreds killed in Watts, Newark, Detroit, and Harlem. But nothing seems more truly red, white and blue Star-Spangled My Country 'Tis of Thee American than three dead and fifty wounded for trying to desegregate a bowling alley. One gets the feeling that if the students had been trying to desegregate two bowling alleys, South Carolina would have dropped the Bomb.

The reaction of whites when they read the news was one of shock, if they had any reaction at all. The reaction of blacks was one of anger. For us it was simply another demonstration by white America that it is working overtime qualifying for the right to be annihilated. We will do our best to oblige.

Perhaps the major reason why it is difficult for whites to communicate with blacks is the inability or refusal of whites to share the anger of blacks. There are many whites who understand the nature of imperialism, oppression, exploitation, and all the other concepts, but their understanding does not give them one of the necessary attributes to make them act on what they intellectualize. That attribute is anger. Anger is not the sustaining force of a revolution, but it is the catalyst many, many times. Blacks are angry, and the Orangeburg Massacre angers even those who have been afraid to be angry. Yet while black anger increases, whites remain only concerned and deeply disturbed. They can analyze what is happening, intellectualize what is happening, but, somehow, what is happening never hits them in the gut. Or if it does, they roll a stick or two, pass it around, and watch the smoke spiral around the posters of Che on their walls. And then they get afraid when blacks, angered at what is being done to them daily, start talking about burning the country down. "I've never done anything against Negroes," they say. "You can't blame me." And in trying to exonerate themselves from all complicity and guilt, they are merely asking, "How can I come out of this alive? How can I save myself?" This is why the black radical reserves his greatest anger for the white who, to all appearances, is most sympathetic to him. Whites are scared for their lives instead of trying to fight for them. That is the difference between whites and blacks today.

A revolutionary knows he has only one thing he can lose by fighting, and that is listening to the beat of his heart. He does not even dare to define this heartbeat as life, because he knows that his life is not his own. Fidel put it well when he said, "What do the dangers or the sacrifices of a man or a nation matter when the destiny of humanity is at stake?" Anyone who wants to be worthy of being remembered as a revolutionary must feel this in every pore of his skin, in every aspect of his being. The destiny of humanity is at stake! There is no other way to think of it. And thinking of it that way, it is clear that there is no middle ground, no way to play the game so you can win the revolution without jeopardizing the beat of your heart. Until whites reach that gut point where they're willing to risk all, then there is no possibility of working with blacks. As

Rap Brown says, "The price of friendship has gone up." In revolution, all must be risked for all to be won.

The struggle will be long and hard and many a heart that now beats will be shattered by a spherical, powder-filled piece of steel. Those who oppress do not respond to petitions, demonstrations, and the demands of the oppressed. The oppressor murders at his leisure and does not cease until the oppressed, recognizing that the oppressor has no right to oppress, assert their right to live by using the only language the oppressor has ever used and the only language that he understands—the sound of gunfire, the sound of dynamite, the sound of his own death in his ear. This is the only lesson to be learned from the Orangeburg Massacre.

FEBRUARY 17, 1968

## THE RIOT COMMISSION REPORT

THE President's Commission on Civil Disorders ("civil disorders" being a euphemism for black uprisings) has come to the startling conclusion that the U.S. is a racist nation. To blacks this is stale news, but nothing that we have ever said about this country has been believed until whites finally got around to saying it. David Walker, Frederick Douglass, Marcus Garvey, W.E.B. DuBois, Malcolm X, LeRoi Jones, Stokely Carmichael, and Rap Brown are only a few of the blacks who have been telling the truth about America.

The commission's report calls white America racist, but it cannot overcome its own racism to at least acknowledge that it had merely reached a conclusion that blacks had been voicing for almost 400 years. The commission report, however, leaves the impression that no one had ever realized the character of America's problem before. And to paraphrase that racist Shakespeare, nothing is so unless white folks think it so. Rap thought it so, and he's in a Louisiana prison cell. His comment on hearing about the report this past weekend was to the point: "The members of the commission should be put in jail under $100,000 bail each, because they're saying essentially what I've been saying."

Be that as it may, the commission report has been headlined all over the country. For months we were treated to little bits and pieces of information here and there that promised something big. "Sources close to the padding in the overstuffed chairs on which the commission members sit say the report is much stronger than anyone had anticipated, etc., etc., etc." Not really. After all, what is the one thing that white folks could say that might give blacks a sense of hope and keep them cool during the summer? To call whites a bunch of racists. This they did, and I guess blacks are now supposed to feel that white folks ain't so bad after all.

Well, the President's commission proves that you have to threaten to kill a man before he'll give your existence minimal recognition. Black oppression is being given serious attention only because the black revolution threatens to destroy the country.

Faced with the threat of destruction, America has a dual reaction: to stockpile weapons in every major city and to offer a program that would, they want us to believe, solve the problems of blacks. These programs have been coming out of Establishment outhouses for the past six months. *Newsweek* magazine devoted practically an entire issue to what must be done. *Fortune* magazine devoted its January issue to what business can do. The Ford Foundation and the Urban Coalition have been working night and day trying to fund anything and everything that would help them preserve their power.

Yet while the commission report is being highly praised,

the Senate can't even pass a civil rights bill to protect civil rights workers, of which there aren't too many any more. And can they honestly expect blacks to have faith in bills any longer? Three boys were murdered and fifty wounded before the Justice Department filed suit against the owner of the bowling alley in Orangeburg, South Carolina. Yet under the 1964 Civil Rights Bill, the Justice Department had the power to act when it was informed of the segregated facility. It chose to act after the massacre had occurred. If every bill that one could dream of were passed by Congress, the reality of black oppression would remain unchanged. And Senator Fred Harris, Democrat of Oklahoma, one of the commission members, admitted he saw little likelihood that Congress or the nation was interested in seriously grappling with the problem. Sociologist Daniel P. Moynihan was another, who after outlining what he thought needed to be done, ended by saying that nothing would be done.

So who is the commission trying to jive with its report? If everyone openly acknowledges that Bloody Summer is on its way, then the commission report can be regarded only as the Establishment's attempt to keep the blood at a minimum during an election year by trying to pacify blacks with militant words.

The commission report might also have the effect of widening the gap between black militants and whites on the left. The former recognize clearly that there is no redress of grievances under the present system; many of the latter feel that the attempt should at least be made. "The government might mean it this time," many whites will say. "At least you should give it the chance." Blacks will call those who say this "a bunch of honkies"; the whites will be hurt and angered and will respond with "Well, if you get shot down, it's your own fault." And the gap will grow a bit more.

No matter how often liberals point to America's fantastic ability to co-opt and to absorb dissidents within its ranks, there is no point of compromise when one reaches an absolutist level. The oppressor can never satisfy the demands of the oppressed when the oppressed begin to fight for liberation. The U.S. makes gestures to reform itself when it is seriously threatened, but reform satisfies only for a time. If every black could be given a new house, a guaranteed annual wage, a car, and a color TV (so I can watch "Mission Impossible"), the fundamental racism in this country would remain untouched. The American system is incapable of touching it.

It is sad to know that the commission's recommendations will not be carried out. While it would leave racism untouched, at least blacks wouldn't have to suffer material deprivation along with racism. While no convincing evidence has come to light that white America actually cares about improving conditions in the ghetto, there is a convincing argument for the government to carry out the commission's recommendations. The effect of those recommendations on the present black liberation struggle if they were carried out might be similar to the effect the 1964 Civil Rights Bill had on the civil rights movement. The passage of the 1964 bill killed the civil rights movement, but not the hunger for liberation. If the commission's recommendations were followed, the present liberation movement might die, but another black liberation movement would surface someplace when it was least expected. Revolution is a process that undulates backward and forward until its forward motion is enough for it to fulfill itself.

There is only one thing an oppressor can do that would

begin to satisfy the oppressed. That is to stop oppressing. This, of course, the oppressor is incapable of doing. And this incapability is what the report of the President's commission is all about.

March 9, 1968

## RIGHT AND WRONG

THE commitment of a revolutionary is found in one basic old-fashioned idea—right and wrong.

For these ultramodern, sophisticated times, to speak of a right and a wrong is to be accused of being simplistic and of being unable to understand the complexities of life. The revolutionary is he who refuses to understand anything except that no man has the right to oppress another and that the oppressed can do no wrong and the oppressor can do no right.

It is wrong that one man should be forced to live his life for the profit of another; it is wrong that children should be hungry (and most of the world's children are); it is wrong that any man, woman, or child should be hungry, without adequate clothing and shelter as long as other men, women, and children have these things. No amount of intellectualizing, theorizing, or reason will make these things right.

There is a class of whites who call themselves liberals,

who will agree with anything a revolutionary may say up to the point of agreeing to what must be done to solve the problem. At that point he "puts his eyes in his pocket and his nose to the ground," as Bob Dylan so graphically described the phenomenon of consciously refusing to see. The white liberal is the Mr. Jones who knows that something is happening and knows what it is and all he can do is become filled with despair. In that state he tries ever more feverishly to breathe life into those dummies that have become symbols of oppression for the oppressed—the vote, Love, Reason, slum rehabilitation, etc. He sees the wrong being committed, but his fear of doing whatever may be necessary is greater than his abhorrence of the wrong. The oppressed have no fear; only a total and complete hatred of wrong and the knowledge that whatever must be done to destroy the wrong must be done.

The white liberal is unable to understand why the black revolutionary has more contempt for him than for a cop. One knows where a cop stands and there is no necessity to even think about it. A cop can be trusted to act like a cop. A liberal can be trusted to act like a liberal, which means that he can't be trusted. There comes a point in a nation's history when events overpower us and we are helpless as we feel ourselves being pushed toward the demarcation line. We feel our lives crumbling before us at the breakfast table. A choice must be made between the forces of oppression and the forces of liberation, and the liberal chooses despair, i.e., oppression. Yet while choosing to make no choice, the liberal continues to mouth the rhetoric of concern, pointing to what is wrong, agonizing over that wrong, and being afraid to pay whatever price is required to kill the wrong. The black militant knows this about the white liberal and hates him, for who is more despicable than the man who knows what is wrong and refuses to act against it?

It would all be infinitely easier if one could say that revolution is an amiable affair that demands very little from its participants. But it isn't. People get hurt, maimed, and killed in revolutions. People starve and the liberal tries to blame the holocaust of revolution on the revolutionary. One such liberal recently told me, "One-third of the nation now lives in poverty. What you propose will result in the entire nation living in poverty much worse than anything which has ever existed in this country." The alternative implied in that answer is that I continue to live in oppression. The liberal denied it and fell into despair, recognizing the inevitability of the oppressed coming alive and saying NO! The oppressed are fanatics about ending oppression; the liberal is as he is named—liberal about ending oppression. He would rather a portion of this nation and the majority of humanity be oppressed. The oppressed would rather all the nation and all of humanity be free. And before that can be, perhaps all will have to suffer. That is a small price to pay for the creation of the New Man.

The time has come when one will choose his friends by what side they are on and the revolutionary has only one friend—a fellow revolutionary. Those who sympathize with the revolution, yet do not do what they can to aid it are as much the enemy as the active counterrevolutionary. Once the oppressed begin fighting the oppressor, there is no compromise. There is only the wrong to be destroyed and the right to be created. The liberal who has always sought to be fair, who has always sought to see both sides of the question, must realize there is only one side. There is no compromise with oppression. From whatever side it is viewed, it can be seen only as wrong.

This is no time for despair. It is a time of joy and exhilaration. The oppressed are coming alive and saying NO! Nothing gives more cause for hope. Nothing could be more beautiful. Everybody's saying they ain't gon' work on Maggie's farm no more.

MARCH 16, 1968

## THE YIPPIES

THE Youth International Party has announced plans to hold a Youth Festival in Chicago at the same time as the Democratic convention. The typical response from most political activists has been on the order of that expressed in the March 4 issue of Students for a Democratic Society's *New Left Notes*.

In an article significantly titled "Don't Take Your Guns to Town," YIP is analyzed and dismissed in two sentences: ". . . their intention to bring thousands of young people to Chicago during the Democratic National Convention to groove on rock bands and smoke grass and then to put them up against bayonets—viewing that as a radicalizing experience—seems manipulative at best. The idea would not be bad, were it not for the Illinois National Guard and the Chicago police." This glib distortion of YIP's intent is shared, unfortunately, by a good many people, who, if they are going to be responsible radicals, cannot afford to so lightly dismiss and refuse to relate to an important political development.

It must be clearly understood that there are many paths to revolution, and in the context of a McLuhanesque America, this becomes increasingly so. (McLuhan's *Understanding Media* should be required reading for all radicals. Marx can wait.) Know your enemy is a primary rule for revolutionaries and knowing how capitalism and imperialism, etc., function does not necessarily mean that you know your enemy. The yippies reflect knowledge of another facet of the enemy—psychological knowledge—and this knowledge is reflected in their style and action. Of course, it is apparent that a lot of activists cannot relate to the yippie style of the constant "put-on" (but is it?), the air of irresponsibility, the seeming lack of any political orientation, and a total and complete lack of seriousness. But as Marshall McLuhan has pointed out so beautifully, the medium is the message and the yippies, in and of themselves, are the message.

On one level they represent what the new left was lamenting a year ago as nonexistent. Well, now it does. Hippies have gone political. (It can be argued that they always were.) But because they aren't talking of grass roots organizing or any of the more traditional approaches to revolution, it is thought that they aren't political. Beyond that, they are articulating the principles of an alternative way of life—a necessary step in any revolution. And most important, perhaps, they address themselves directly to people, not with words but action. "The only vanguard is the vanguard in action," Jerry Rubin, one of the most articulate revolutionaries in the country and a founder of YIP, has said. "All those hundreds of hours of bullshit meetings were just that—bullshit." We've all sat in more meetings than we can count and have come away tired, demoralized and entertaining thoughts of joining the Air Force or the WACS, just to get the taste of the meeting out of our mouths. And all of us are veterans of picket lines, marches, and demonstrations, and we left them so frustrated and angry that we felt like kicking trash cans and little kids. "What's needed is a new generation of nuisances, a new generation of people who are freaky, crazy, irrational, sexy, angry, irreligious, childish, and mad . . . people who burn draft cards, people who burn dollar bills, people who burn M.A. and doctoral degrees . . . people who lure the youth with music, pot, and LSD, people who proudly carry Vietcong flags . . . people who say fuck on television . . . people who have nothing material to lose but their bodies."

The yippies represent psychological guerrilla warfare. They created stark fear when they went to the Stock Exchange and threw dollar bills from the gallery on to the floor during the peak trading hours. They've run through the streets of New York yelling "The war is over!" Into stores and out, "The war is over! The war is over!" In a country where the picket sign, march, and demonstration have become respectable, other means of communicating a political point of view must be found. Regis Debray talks of armed propaganda, which is exemplified in this country by the Deacons and Huey Newton and the Black Panther Party for Self-Defense. The yippies have begun to explore the techniques of disarming propaganda. They have their roots not in Mao or Che, but in the Provos, rock, and Lenny Bruce. They ignore what a man thinks and grab him by the balls to communicate their message. They seek to involve people in an experience, not argue with them. They are like Zen monks, who never answered a question directly, never set forth a list of Do's and Don'ts, Rights and Wrongs, but answered a student's question with a hard slap. The yippies are a hard slap, a kick in the crotch, a bunch of snipers pinning the enemy down and making him afraid to move.

The yippies are aiming their festival not at the Democratic convention, as the other political organizations will be doing, but at the youth, at those more than 100,000 teenagers who ran away from home last summer, going on strike against the way of life America was presenting them through their parents. The yippie festival presents an alternative. Embodied in the festival will be the values for another way of living, just as the liberated zones of Vietnam present an alternative way of life to the Vietnamese peasant. And once you've lived in a liberated zone, you'll fight to keep it from being reclaimed. The yippies are a liberated zone. Revolution is the experience that revolutionizes and it is not successful until it has involved the greatest number of people in action that revolutionizes them. This is the intent of the yippie festival.

It is all too easy to reject the yippies without ever understanding their value. They do not have the complete answer, nor do they claim to. But they represent one level of activity that is essential. They may not represent your particular "bag." Fine, but they are too important to be rejected, as so many who consider themselves political have done.

MARCH 30, 1968

# THE DEATH OF MARTIN LUTHER KING, JR.

ONLY the death of John F. Kennedy has created as much public attention as the death of Martin Luther King, Jr. In both deaths there was the feeling that something more than the life of an individual had ended. In both deaths shock and sorrow were felt, but underneath the "Oh, no!," there was the sense of fear, of being afraid of what was to come, and the guilt at realizing, yet once again, exactly what America is.

This fear and guilt have led to the vulgarities that have been spewing forth since King's murder. The same people who were criticizing King for the Memphis rebellion a week prior to his death, the same people who were demanding that he call off his planned Poor People's March in Washington, were now lamenting his death, extolling him as a great American, as a great leader of his people. It was vulgar because it was so obvious that the tears being shed were not for Martin Luther King but for white America. Lyndon Johnson appeared on television before King's corpse was cold and read a statement asking blacks to refrain from "blind violence." What unmitigated arrogance! Did he consider the violence his administration was unleashing upon the Vietnamese at the very moment he was speaking to be "clear-sighted" violence?

Yet, while Johnson and government officials from coast to coast called for nonviolence, National Guardsmen were being sent into Memphis and police departments across the country were getting out their shiny new weapons. While public officials praised the teachings and life's work of Martin King, they exhibited their faith in the man and what he represented by sending their armed forces into the "colonies."

In death as in life, however, Martin Luther King continued to fulfill his role. As a "leader," King was not an organizer or a political theoretician. His activities always had a faint smell of opportunism about them, as he moved into areas to organize mass demonstrations after others had done the groundwork. He always seemed a bit at a loss as to what to do, besides preach nonviolence and beg white America to change. He was not a leader, but a symbol. He put himself forward as the touchstone against which America could judge itself. And time after time, America came up losing. Each massive demonstration King organized uncovered another layer of racism and hate in white America. The liberals supported King with talk and money, but they left it to him to civilize white people. They quieted their consciences by their verbal and monetary support. After the Chicago demonstrations in the summer of 1966, King was somewhat despondent and remarked privately, "I think I made one mistake. I underestimated the depths of hate in America." Believing that America would respond to nonviolence, he made America show its true face. That is not what he had set out to do, but that was the result. Those of us who were younger had known for some time that there was no hope within America's present context. King provided the proof and Malcolm X, Stokely Carmichael and Rap Brown came along to provide the analysis and rhetoric. They presented the evidence that King uncovered and refused to believe. As an individual, King was a large figure on the American scene, but it is in his role as the unconscious and unwilling instrument of the forces of history that his real significance lies.

Since his murder, the arrogance of white America has never been more evident. The same Lyndon Johnson and Hubert Humphrey who a few short weeks ago were denying the truth of the Riot Commission Report are now calling for action along the lines of the commission's proposals. The same people who hated King, because he brought people into the street, ordered flags flown at half-staff and felt good, because who could ever remember flags being at half-staff over the death of a Negro, "the grandson of a slave," as the Columbia Broadcasting System's Eric Sevareid said, telling white folks how good they were. Oh, how they love Martin King now, because he was the buffer between them and us—the blacks for whom nonviolence is an exercise in masochism. (Dr. King cared about the soul of America. We care about the soul of the oppressed and recognize that America's soul is what is oppressing us.) They are weeping for Martin Luther King, because in the shot that killed him they heard the shots that will eventually kill them. They hated King's assassin, because they understood so well that King was the white man's best friend. Perhaps his only friend. They understood it, though, in the report of that rifle, not from King's words and dreams.

But Martin Luther King was redeemed, not in the lowered flags or the eulogies, but in the smoke drifting over the White House, in the more than twenty cities where blacks took the streets. King was redeemed in a manner that he was opposed to and didn't understand, but the "young bloods" in the street understood. Martin Luther King was a "brother," a member of the family, whom you disagreed with, fought with, but when it got down to the nitty-gritty, you defended. Blacks were incredulous on hearing of King's murder. He played the game by their rules. He believed in America as if he were one of the signers of the Constitution. He loved America as if he had sewn the first flag. And he articulated a dream for America more forcefully than any man since Thomas Jefferson. And this was the man that was now dead.

Now that he is, America will go through a period of guilt that may outdo the guilt shown during the civil rights movement in the early 1960's. That guilt may bring on a rash of social and economic programs, all in the name of Martin Luther King. But we are tired of the bloodstained hands trying to smother us in an embrace of brotherhood. We don't want any flags flown at half-staff when we die and we sure don't want the goddam President coming to our funeral. If any flags are to be flown, they will be the new flags we'll fly over their corpses. And there'll be no funerals to attend. Only victory festivals.

We share the same dream that Martin Luther King so

poetically articulated, but it is from the ashes that the phoenix will rise. That is not the way he would have wanted it to be. But it was he whom history used to show us that that is the way America will have it be.

APRIL 13, 1968

# THE FUNERAL OF MARTIN LUTHER KING, JR.

IT was an exercise in extreme masochism to sit before the television set and for seven hours watch the funeral of Martin Luther King, Jr. Dr. King was fortunate in that respect. He missed it.

The ordeal came not from the fact that he was dead and this was his funeral. The murder of black men and black women and black children is an American cliché, and Dr. King was simply another one. A prominent one, obviously, but still a cliché.

The ordeal came from being subjected to the racism of the television commentators. It was a good example of that unconscious racism which white people can somehow never become conscious of. It was the kind of racism that is involved when a white activist says to a black person, in a matter-of-fact way: "Yeah, man. I'm thinking about going to Europe. I just can't stand this country anymore." And of course, the black person, who has hated America more deeply and longer, who can't afford to go to Europe, who even if he could knows that one doesn't run to the original home of the honky to get away from the one here, simply jots the honky's name down in his little black mental notebook of people to kill by slow torture on that Great Day. Yet the white activist can't understand that. One can respect him who says, "I am your enemy." ("Solid. We got something in common, 'cause I hate you, too.") But he who says he stands with you in the revolutionary struggle is the one to be most aware of, because when the deal goes down, he might be in Europe. (Pan Am makes the going great.)

In the rush of white America to expunge its sins in the blood of Dr. King, it forgot that he was black, that he had such an appeal to the black community because his rhetoric and his style came from his roots in the black community of the Baptist Church and chicken-eating preachers and the undertaker's fans you tried to cool yourself with on hot Southern Baptist Church Sunday mornings. They forgot all that and thought it was sufficient to acknowledge that which could not be denied—Dr. King was Negro. And they acknowledged it by always showing on the television screens that so many "notables" had come to the funeral of this "Negro."

From looking at television it seemed that the only people who attended King's funeral were Gene McCarthy, the Kennedys, Richard Nixon, et al. Yet the overwhelming majority of the 1,300 people inside the church were black, members of the church who knew Dr. King in a way that others didn't. But these people weren't important. Nothing should strengthen one's will to live as much as the fact that Nixon, Kennedy and McCarthy might come to your funeral. And don't say it can't happen. It's only after you're dead that those who hated you can really get to you. Those who loved you become shadows in the background.

There were other "notables" there, we were told. Harry Belafonte, Sammy Davis, Marlon Brando, and Paul Newman. O.K., but the real notables of the black community did not get even the slightest nod of recognition from the TV cameras. Aretha Franklin was there. So were Diana Ross and The Supremes, Stevie Wonder, Nancy Wilson, Mrs. Betty Shabbazz, Eartha Kitt, Barbara McNair and Bill Cosby. These were some of the names that were important for blacks, but the television commentators didn't mention them for the simple reason that, like the people in the church, they weren't important. And it was amusing the way any mention of Stokely Carmichael's presence at the funeral was avoided.

What hurt most of all was that it could have been so easily avoided had black commentators been used. White folks want us to believe they're serious about straightening things out and they can't even find a black news commentator for the funeral of a prominent black man. It hurt to have to listen to a white man make inane and irrelevant comments about something which blacks know intimately. To white commentators Dr. King was never more than good copy. They were reporting a "historic event." A black commentator would've reported the souls of black folks. One really wanted to cry watching Dr. King go down to his final burying ground to the accompaniment of vacuities muttered by white commentators who didn't know him, didn't feel anything for him, and really didn't care.

Saddest of all is the fact that they don't realize what they did or even that they did anything. The white power structure is trying to cram the memory of Dr. King down the throat of black America. The white liberal is trying to say that he was theirs and that any black person who does not honor his memory by turning the cheek to the inevitable blows is dishonoring him. And neither understands that no matter how much nonviolence Dr. King talked, he was ours. We were angered by his murder. White America was only saddened. And that shows how deep the racism goes. If white folks want us to believe that they are serious about revolution, then they'll have to start getting angry when a black is murdered. In case they hadn't noticed, we stopped crying a long time ago. And black men, women, and children are murdered every day. It's just that their names aren't King.

It's unfair to hate a man for being unconscious of his racism. Yet his cries of "But I didn't know" will not save his life on the day of Reckoning.

April 20, 1968

# LEADERSHIP IN THE MOVEMENT

AN atmosphere of enthusiasm for revolution (which is different from revolutionary enthusiasm) has been created among us. While enthusiasm is good, uncritical enthusiasm can cause us to delude ourselves into thinking that we are stronger than we actually are and that the enemy is weaker than he actually is.

Revolution cannot be called forth by the constant chanting of its name. But the sound may deafen our ears to the marching feet of a militaristic fascist state that will come under the guise of liberalism. That is more likely to come in the near future than the revolutionary flag from every flagpole. We must have faith that the revolution will eventually triumph, but we act irresponsibly if we let that faith be expressed in such clichés as, "The revolutionary struggle cannot be defeated." Maybe it can't, but it can sure be hurt badly. Victory does not proceed from blind faith. It comes only from knowing the right thing to do at the right time and doing it.

The success of a revolution depends to a great degree upon the quality of the revolutionary leadership. That leadership articulates the goals of the revolution, the methods by which those goals will be attained, while at the same time embodying the ideals of the revolution itself. Those upon whom the revolutionary leadership falls assume an awesome responsibility. There is none higher, for the words and actions of the revolutionary leader must always advance the revolutionary consciousness and revolutionary effectiveness of the people. The revolutionary leader can never "shuck" and "jive."

In recent weeks, much of the leadership of the white antiwar movement and the black liberation movement has been "shucking" and "jiving" at the most critical time in the life of our infant revolutionary struggle.

The adult leadership of the white antiwar movement has always vacillated between liberalism (antiwar moralizing) and radicalism (anti-imperialism). It has vacillated between seeing the war in Vietnam as the issue and seeing the war as the most immediate issue by which people could be politicized about the nature of this government. (The war in Vietnam means more than that people are being killed.) The adult leadership of the antiwar movement vacillates no more. The candidacies of Senators Eugene McCarthy and Robert Kennedy and President Johnson's withdrawal have shown it to be firmly liberal. This leadership announced that the antiwar movement had moved from protest to resistance. Yet this very leadership has been unable to resist McCarthy and Kennedy. It has not been able to see how McCarthy and Kennedy can be used to educate people beyond a stage of protest that was based on moral outrage.

Most indicative is the presence of New York's Mayor John V. Lindsay at the April 27 antiwar demonstration. There is nothing wrong with Mayor Lindsay's being opposed to the war. However, our opposition to the war also brings us into opposition to Lindsay, McCarthy, and Kennedy. They would not be opposing the war if it were succeeding. It is the failure of the war which they are opposed to, and not the ends it was hoped the war would accomplish.

If the adult leaders of the antiwar movement think they can use the liberal opposition to the war for their own ends, they are mistaken. McCarthy and Kennedy have given the liberals new strength. Lindsay's presence at the April 27 demonstration will only increase that strength. Coalitions between liberals (those who believe that solutions can be found within the framework of the system) and radicals (those who believe that the system cannot provide real solutions) are always dangerous for radicals if the radicals do not represent the greater strength.

Ultimately there can be no coalition between conflicting ideologies. The ideology of liberalism is merely the ideology of oppression and exploitation with perfume on. The only difference between the liberal and the conservative is in the choice of weapons—an M-16 rather than a Stoner gun. The leadership of the antiwar movement created an enthusiasm for radical change in white youth. The youth took the leadership away from it at the Pentagon last October.

The leadership of the black movement has always been more radical than that of the antiwar movement and whatever can be pointed to as a white radical movement. However, the black movement in its enthusiasm has had a tendency toward militant-sounding rhetoric. Militant rhetoric has its place, but it is not a substitute for revolutionary principle. Sometimes militant rhetoric is nothing more than a cover-up for a lack of revolutionary thought. In recent weeks, some militant black leaders have acted in ways which lead one to wonder if they are as revolutionary as we have been led to think.

Most disturbing has been the response of black leadership to the imprisonment of Rap Brown. For two months the government held Rap in prison, and those black leaders with the most influence didn't do what they could have done. Why did they not go to New Orleans and organize demonstrations to bring pressure to bear for Rap's release? The black colleges in that city were ready for just such action, and action in New Orleans would have created action elsewhere in the country. The black leadership did little to see that Rap's imprisonment was nothing more than a waste of time, precious time.

After Dr. King's murder, why did many black leaders find it "revolutionary" either to go into the streets with guns or go into the streets, in some instances with members of the white power structure, and urge the people to "cool it"? There was a revolutionary alternative. Knowing that black people were going to respond to King's murder by taking the streets, the most influential black leaders could have put forward the following proposition to the government: Release Rap Brown in twenty-four hours and prove to black people that you mean some of this garbage you're talking about justice and freedom and we'll do all we can to keep the brothers and sisters "cool." If the government had released Rap, it would have been a definite victory. If it had not, the political content of the rebellions would have been doubled and the revolutionary consciousness of black people immeasurably raised. Instead, militant-sounding rhetoric was used when revolutionary action was possible.

The government held Rap in jail for two months. It now knows that it can jail any black leader it wants to and there will be little more than a murmur coming from the black militant leadership. The black movement will pay many times over for letting the government hold Rap for two months.

Just as the candidacies of McCarthy and Kennedy have put liberals in the position where they can take control of the antiwar movement, the assassination of Dr. King has put them, black and white liberals, into a position where they can take over a good segment of the black movement, isolate the most radical part, and eliminate it quietly.

A revolution cannot surpass the quality of its leadership. The enemy was momentarily thrown off-balance by the strong opposition of black and white youth. Now the enemy has regained the offensive. Unfortunately, the leadership of the white antiwar movement and the black liberation movement still think the enemy is running for its life. It is they who are running and are dragging a good many followers with them. To sound militant is not necessarily to be revolutionary. Perhaps the time has come for these leaders to re-examine themselves and become truly revolutionary or be replaced. "Shucking" and "jiving" leaders cannot be tolerated when the destiny of humanity is at stake.

April 27, 1968

## ON BECOMING REVOLUTIONARY

FOR there to be a revolution, it is not enough to desire and work for the destruction of one system and the rise of another. The desired revolution might not come to pass if those who wish the revolution to come about do not recognize and kill in themselves all of the habits and values and thought patterns of the undesirable society. Once this is done, it is then necessary to begin to live the values and think in the patterns that will be the creative multi-rhythms of the new society.

At present, it is clear that if there were a revolution anytime soon, nothing would change, because most of us continue to think in the ways we have been taught. It is only our words that are different. To change America, we must cease to react, respond, and even feel as Americans. America has programed us constantly since the days of our separate births. And even after we become conscious of the "system," "neocolonialism," "imperialism," and "revolution," we remain programed. Thus, our actions and our words have a monotonous constancy, and it is no problem for the enemy to deal with us.

The antiwar movement has always been concerned with semiannual demonstrations of thousands upon thousands. At the beginning this was necessary because strength could be shown only by having the greatest number of bodies together in one place and at one time. However, a point is reached when sheer numbers of bodies mean nothing in and of themselves. The U.S. government gives us a "body count" of "enemy" dead every day. It has no other way of assessing its effort. The antiwar movement gives us a "body count" of demonstrators, and we are led to believe that this gives us an assessment of our strength. The only thing that the demonstration "body count" tells us is that the antiwar movement has been influenced by the Gallup Poll mentality that rules America. Too often we get involved in a numbers game and forget that our goal is not to count "heads," but to involve those "heads" in meaningful action. But we get so involved in turning out large numbers that we forget about involving those numbers in anything significant. To be only a number in a "body count" is not to be significant, and perhaps this is the reason so many leave the mass demonstrations feeling dissatisfied and frustrated. Perhaps it has never occurred to any of us that our goal, in fact, is to win, and everything that does not point toward that winning is irrelevant and immaterial.

We have also made the error of overemphasizing the mass media as being necessary to our winning. Lenin, Ho, and Mao managed to be rather effective without holding one press conference. Yet because we have been raised in an age of mass media and know most of what we know through the mass media, we react as we have been programed whenever we have to convey information to a large number of people. And if our demonstration was not reported on the six o'clock news or did not make the first three pages of the paper, we feel that our action was a failure and cry that the media are conspiring against us. Of course they are. To cry out against press distortions is like going to bed with a rattlesnake and reacting with pained surprise when the rattlesnake bites you. Ultimately the only means of communication that the revolutionary organization can rely upon are cadres of revolutionary organizers. Too often we rely upon press releases and newspaper ads to communicate. We realize, of course, that a press release and a newspaper ad are read by the enemy as well as our friends. Yet we rationalize the thought away. Somehow we find the greatest value in announcing what we are going to do rather than in simply doing it.

A recent example of this was the Anti-Imperialist Feeder March in New York City on April 27. Several radical organizations withdrew from the main antiwar demonstration scheduled for that day. They announced that they would hold their own demonstration and refuse to apply for a police permit. "The Streets Belong to the People" was their slogan. They were correct in every regard except one. They announced that all demonstrators were to assemble in Washington Square at a particular hour. Once that announcement was made, it was clear that the demonstration would never get started because the police would have assembled there before them. The result was simple: The police had a good time cracking heads and arresting people.

There are some radical organizations, white and black, that reflect their American upbringing by always wanting a confrontation with the police. The U.S. forces in Vietnam are always complaining that the guerrillas won't come out and "fight like men." And we reflect the same thought patterns when we think we should confront the police, that we should stand up and "fight like men." Common sense tells us that you can't go up against the police in a head-on confrontation and win. But we have been psyched by the American code which says that you shouldn't hit a man when his back is turned. As long as the U.S. government has the Army, Air Force, Navy, Marines, FBI, CIA and police departments like those in Chicago and New York, it is clear that the only time to strike is when backs are turned. As Chairman Mao put it: "The enemy's rear is our front."

Last week the government announced that a National Riot Control Center had been established in the Pentagon. That should tell us one thing—the time for "rioting" has come to an end. If you didn't get your TV set last summer, you can forget it now. The "man" was courteous enough to announce that he is preparing to deal with mass rebellions. Then it is time to stop rebelling en masse. It is time to think tactically. It is time to think how to achieve the maximum effect with the minimum effort and risk. It is time to think how to use the maximum number of people with the minimum concentration of those people in one place. It is time to think.

We cannot help it if we are Americans. We cannot expect to win, however, if we continue to be Americans. We must become "those who have transformed themselves"—revolutionaries.

May 4, 1968

## LEARNING FROM MISTAKES

THE revolutionary is an idealist and a pragmatist. His motivation for being a revolutionary is, in the end, the ideal of creating the New Man. He recognizes, however, that the New Man is not born, wholly formed, from the revolution. That New Man is created by some blood, a lot of tears, and constant sweat. The creation of this ideal demands that the revolutionary do whatever may be necessary. Sometimes it is necessary to proceed with militancy. Other times it is necessary to proceed with caution. And sometimes it is necessary to pause and see where you've been so you can better go where you want to go.

The time to pause has come. In eight years the black movement has come from nonviolent sit-ins to talk of urban guerrilla warfare. That is a lot of ground to cover in such a short period of time. (And everybody hasn't covered the same ground.) During the past eight years, mistakes have been made. Mistakes are unavoidable, but they aren't fatal if they are brought to light, examined, and the weaknesses which created them destroyed.

One of the major weaknesses of the radical black movement for the past year or so has been its use of militant rhetoric. To talk militantly and to act militantly are not necessarily revolutionary. Sometimes what is called militancy may endanger the revolution more than help it. Militant rhetoric which cannot be supported by militant action is misleading and dishonest. It brings forth expectations from the people which cannot be fulfilled. At the same time, it can unite the enemy and force him to unleash his power before you are capable of dealing with it.

Militant rhetoric has its place. In the initial stages, it is invaluable as an awakener of the people. The enunciation of the concept of black power did just that. However, militant rhetoric is always a dangerous tool, for it can so quickly and so easily begin to devour all who use it and all who listen. It feels so good when it comes from the tongue and it sounds so good as it enters the ear. If used without discretion, it can become a thing to be loved for itself. Thus, because of their militant rhetoric and personal charisma, some radical black leaders have become "happenings," not revolutionaries.

To call whites "a bunch of honkies" does not necessarily reflect revolutionary understanding. To say that "black is beautiful" (and undeniably it is) says little, because blackness is not sufficient for revolutionary purposes. (Hubert Humphrey told an audience several weeks ago that he was a "soul brother." Undoubtedly, sometime during his campaign, Hubert will find it expedient to extol the virtues of blackness.)

The militant rhetoric of the radical black movement has had a profound effect on the black community. However, the militancy of this rhetoric was mistakenly called "revolutionary." It was not. It did, however, help lay the foundation for the black community to become truly revolutionary.

At the same time, this rhetoric has served to organize white nationalism. The domestic arms buildup is now common knowledge. The stage has been set for a confrontation between blacks and whites, and it is a confrontation which blacks cannot win. You can yell "Black Power" and "Honky" down the barrel of a tank's gun if you want to, but it ain't gon' be too effective. If you're a 97-pound weakling, you don't jump up and talk about whipping the "front four" of the Green Bay Packers. You wait until you've put on some muscle, figured out the best way to deal with the situation, then you take care of business.

The revolutionary's concern is not to sound or be militant. (A militant is not necessarily a revolutionary.) His concern is to be realistic. The revolutionary is very careful not to do anything that would call for a confrontation between him and the enemy as long as he knows he can't win that confrontation. The revolutionary does nothing that will serve only to unite the enemy against him. The longer he can keep the conservatives and liberals (both enemies) fighting each other, the more time he has to get his thing together. It is worth quoting Fidel Castro as he talks about why the Cuban revolutionaries did not announce a radical program when they first went to the mountains: ". . . to have stated a radical program at that moment would have resulted in aligning against the revolution all the most reactionary forces, which were then divided. It would have caused the formation of a solid front among the North

American imperialists, Batista, and the ruling classes. They would have called finally upon the troops of the United States to occupy the country." Given the means of the Cuban Rebel Army at that time, this would have spelled almost certain defeat, or at least a much longer and bloodier struggle.

Given the lack of organization and means of the radical black movement, much of it stands in danger of being annihilated. At this point there is not much that can be done to avoid that. But revolutions are not built in a week or in eight years. To quote Fidel once again: "No one is born a revolutionary. A revolutionary is formed through a process . . . Ultimately a revolutionary struggle is like a military war. You have to set for yourself only those goals that are attainable at a given moment. The fight depends on the correlation of forces, on a series of circumstances, and every revolutionary must propose for himself all the objectives that are possible within the correlation of forces and within the circumstances in which he acts."

The radical black movement has given birth to that revolutionary process. Part of that process is learning our faults. Learning them, we proceed to correct them. And having corrected them, we once again move forward.

May 18, 1968

# REACTIONARY ASPECTS OF BLACK POWER

BLACK POWER! As a slogan, it was a clarion call, awakening the dead and giving life to the unborn. Prior to Black Power, Freedom Now was the cry, but even the truest of believers knew that Freedom wasn't about to come Now or any other time in the foreseeable future. Freedom Now was a plea elevated to a demand which gave strength to those demanding, but failed to move those at whom the demand was flung. Black Power was aggressive, tough, and uncompromising. Basically, the words were a psychological weapon, giving strength to those who yelled them and fear to those who heard.

As a concept, Black Power was more ambiguous. Literally, it meant power for black people, and everyone had his own definition of what that power was to consist and how it was to be obtained. Within the radical black community, Black Power eventually came to mean black control of black communities, the exclusion of whites from black organizations, meetings, etc., and pride in blackness and black culture. Through Black Power, blacks asserted their right to speak for themselves, define for themselves, and organize themselves.

It took many white liberals and radicals some time to recuperate from the shock. Eventually, however, most realized the necessity and desirability of Black Power. The Establishment didn't reflect on the necessity or the desirability, but eventually bowed to the inevitability and began searching for new ways to maintain its control over the black community. This took some time, for even the most dedicated member of the Establishment found it difficult to endure the constant mortar barrages of "Honky!," "Whitey!," and so forth. The ability to adjust, however, is one reason the Establishment has been able to maintain and extend its power. The Establishment adjusted to this new phenomenon and began hunting for the weaknesses of the Black Power movement. It found them. Black Power got stuck on Black and didn't move on to Power.

Perhaps this was inevitable. When a people have been oppressed on the basis of color and race, they have to use their color and race as a weapon to liberate themselves. A man who sees himself only as a reflection in the eyeballs of another is not a man. The colonized must kill themselves and awaken the unborn within before they can address themselves directly to the colonizer. Thus, the natural hair styles, the African dress, the emphasis on black culture were the reclaiming of the self. The expression of a hatred of whites was another aspect of the reclamation. It is impossible for the oppressed not to hate the oppressor. However, it is not always expedient for the oppressed to tell the oppressor. Black Power said, forget the expediency and lay it on the line. And without a doubt, it has definitely been laid on the line. However, there is a possibility that the radical black movement may be lying on the line, pinned down by that which it has laid.

The liberal establishment realized that as long as blacks were talking about blackness, as long as blacks were cussing white folks, as long as blacks were only reclaiming themselves, they were not the threat which they could be. A threat did not exist until blacks moved from blackness to an understanding of White Power (the system) and organized to destroy it. Suddenly the Establishment began seeing a virtue in blackness and began encouraging it, as did even funding groups, whose programs were essentially cultural. Too many blacks thought that having won the right to assert their blackness meant more than it actually did. Blackness became an end to be achieved, when in actuality blackness is only the starting point. It is one weapon in the liberation struggle. For too many blacks it has become the struggle itself.

The principal beneficiaries of Black Power have been the black middle class. Jobs have opened up to professional blacks. Black college students have won their fight for black courses as a part of the curriculum in white and black colleges. (Yale University is even going so far as to offer a major in Afro-American studies.) It is in the area of education that Black Power has had an enormous impact. Black parents have demanded, and in some instances gotten across the necessity for, black consciousness to be reflected in the teaching in ghetto schools.

Whites have been educated to a realization of their racism to the point where it is almost a cliché for whites to confess publicly just how racist they are. Sometimes it can get rather sickening, but at least consciousness exists where yesterday there was none. It is part of the process.

Those who have benefited least from Black Power, however, are those whose needs are the most acute—the black poor. They have gained pride and self-respect, but unlike the black intelligentsia, there has been no opportunity for them to parlay this new pride and self-respect into something more concrete. The black poor have rebelled and taken to the streets to gain a measure of that which has been denied them. But many recognize that one's life is a helluva price to pay for a TV set, a suit, or a fifth of whiskey. And too many black people have been shot down in the streets by cops who have no trouble believing that a bottle of Scotch is worth more than a human being.

Black Power has addressed itself to racism, but not to the other part of the picture—exploitation. The black radical movement has spoken of black control of black communities, and while this sounds good, it is naïve. As long as the black community exists within the capitalist community, it is impossible for blacks to control it. The Establishment has reached the point where it will allow blacks to run the black community. That has become expedient. To administrate, however, is not to control. And in the end, it is irrelevant who controls the black community as long as that community exists within a capitalist structure.

The energy unleashed by Black Power has too long been directed against a false enemy. It is too easy to blame "the white man" for all troubles. In the end, that is a cop-out. Maybe the white man is the enemy, but if we awoke in the morning to find that white people had suddenly disappeared, little would be changed. If blacks were in the saddle, their blackness alone would be no guarantee that they wouldn't ride the horse the same way whites have.

But many blacks see the struggle as black against white. Perhaps it is, but if that is true, then nothing really matters. It is not enough to love black people and hate white people. That is therapy, not revolution. It is incumbent upon the revolutionary that he not do to someone else what that someone may have done to him. It is all too easy for the oppressed to become the oppressor. No matter how delicious it might feel, it is a feeling the oppressed have to deny themselves.

The revolutionary is he who loves humanity and hates injustice. It is only through a commitment of this kind that social change in America will result in Revolution and not in another of the infinite varieties of oppression.

May 25, 1968

## RUMORS

FOR anyone involved in the movement, it is common to hear rumors of various sorts almost daily. These rumors extend all the way from supposed "inside" information about a meeting held in the inner recesses of the Pentagon to who's really sleeping with whom. Fortunately most of these rumors are harmless, for if they weren't, it is doubtful if the movement could have survived this long.

Periodically the grapevine jumps with the news that "so-and-so is an agent." Allegations of this kind are spread quickly and with a certain joy. Western society inoculates us with an enthusiasm for any kind of "bad" news. We race to the telephone to share with a friend bad news of someone's downfall. "Heard about Roy? . . . You didn't . . . Wow, man! Where you been? . . . Well, he sliced up his ol' lady and the fuzz caught him trying to stuff her body between the pages of the *Quotations from Chairman Mao* . . . Yeah, he must've really flipped out this time . . ." And, of course, the listener to this conversation can barely wait to call up somebody else.

In the meantime, Roy is sitting around his apartment with his ol' lady listening to Bob Dylan. That night when Roy and his ol' lady hit the block, it is immediately apparent that Roy's ol' lady has not been laid between the pages of Chairman Mao's wisdom. Everybody will have a good laugh and that will be that. Yet, if another rumor about Roy started making the rounds a few days later, it would be spread as quickly as the previous one.

We are so quick to believe the worst about each other. How could anyone who has had any contact with Carl Oglesby, whether in person or through his writings or lectures, believe that he was working for Bobby Kennedy? Yet this rumor was rampant earlier this spring and few seemed to question it. Instead, there was much more interest and enthusiasm in spreading it. No irreparable damage has been done to Oglesby's reputation, but only because the rumor was so innocuous.

The eagerness of movement people to spread any and all rumors makes the movement that much more vulnerable to exploitation by government agents. It becomes a simple matter for an FBI infiltrator to accuse a leader or potential leader of an organization of being an agent, and with everyone's eagerness to believe it, the accusation is flung far and wide, and the movement has lost a valuable person. In the early 1960's, a member of the Communist Party was expelled when another member accused him of being an agent. Six months later it was discovered that the accuser was the agent.

For the accused, it is an impossible situation. How can one prove that he is not an agent? It is as difficult a task as proving that someone is an agent. But the mere allegation is too often taken as proof in itself.

During the days of Joe McCarthy, to say that a person was a Communist was enough literally to wreck that person's life. The movement is not in any danger at present of succumbing to the kind of hysteria that prevailed during the McCarthy period, but the seeds of a McCarthyism do exist within the movement. And they are seeds which must not be allowed to take root.

This kind of situation can be guarded against very easily by simply asking whoever is spreading the rumor for proof. That is generally enough to end the conversation, for the usual proof is, "Well, I heard . . ." Actions are proof. Not words.

It is vital that every person in the movement act responsibly at all times. Being responsible means being eager to stop gossip, not listen to it and spread it. If one's revolutionary commitment is not strong enough to stop gossip, then one's own sense of self-preservation should be. One day the gossip and the rumors might be about you.

In the outside world one is taught to be responsible only to himself and for himself (and his employer). In the movement we must be responsible to and for each other. In the present absence of geographical liberated zones, we must represent psychic zones of liberation wherever we are. We cannot look upon or react to each other as we did before we got involved in the movement. We begin, thereby, to create the new society as we fight for the destruction of the present one.

June 8, 1968

## NOT IN MEMORY OF ROBERT KENNEDY

MAYBE one day the nation will go into mourning
when poverty penetrates the skull of a poor
man and shatters his brain.

Maybe one day the flags will be lowered, the
schools closed and a day of mourning proclaimed
when the pain of every morning's sunrise
makes the heartbeats of black mothers stumble
through the bare kitchens of their lives.

Maybe one day television stations will cancel their
regular programs to show us film clips of the
important events in these everyday everyminute
lives.

and we can sit in front of our television sets and watch
the deceased
when he was called "Spic!" by his teacher,

when he was told to get off the corner by a cop
  on a hot summer night,
when he went to work shining shoes washing dishes
  selling newspapers on the subway
running numbers hustling hustling hustling
when he got busted for being too slow in moving
  off the corner because the poor have
no reason to move fast.
when he went through all those circles of
  America the Inferno
which Richard Wright James Baldwin Claude
  Brown Howling Wolf Joe Tex Ray Charles
have described for white people crackers honkies.

we can sit in front of our television sets and watch the life of the deceased
unwind in its interminable monotonous relentless unwinding
through the sun-burnt vineyards of
  California
through the sun-tormented cotton fields of
  Mississippi
through the sun-cursed streets of
  Harlem
through the sun-slapped valleys of Appalachia.

(There was no touch football
on sun-kissed rolling lawns
for the deceased

There was no frolicking
on sun-swept Hyannis Port beaches

for the deceased.

There was no skiing
on sun-curved Aspen Colorado slopes
for the deceased.
He had no shock of hair curving his brow
and women didn't shriek when he grinned
and no one ever wanted to vote him in office for
anything.
Not for anything at all.)
But we can watch him on our television screens
as he tried to bring to himself
what TIME LIFE LOOK NBCBSABClairol The
Dodge REBELLION
tell him are the source of all happiness and
all good things.

and into the tiny livingsleepingfucking arguing-room of
his one-room shack
three-room tenement
he brings a 24″ television set over-stuffed reclining
chair sofa stereophonic console wife four children
another coming several thousand roaches fifteen
rats procreating more rapidly even than he but a lot
easier to feed because they love the young
tender milk-drenched flesh of children.

We will watch him and will see nothing that we have
not seen before
on the TV SPECIALS on "Poverty."
We will see nothing that we have not seen before
since we became aware that there is

an other america
and
why
rap brown is
and
most people resent the knowing.

There will never be a national day of mourning
for the assassination of a poor man
because
poor men are assassinated every day.
the American Way of Life causes constant massive
hemorrhaging in the brain,
but the victim never dies.
he just keeps on living until one day he picks up a gun
and fires it at his oppressor
and casts his vote for liberation.
sirhan bishara sirhan.

And America wonders why
while we say now
and the President appoints a Commission on
Violence
while the Vietnamese show us how.

the martyr is not he who was killed,
but he who fired the gun.

That is all we need to remember about the sixth day of
june nineteen hundred and sixty-eight.

June 15, 1968

# POLITICAL MEANING OF THE DEATH OF RFK

AS a political ideology, liberalism stands in the middle between conservatism and radicalism, and is, in actuality, a diluted amalgam of both. The liberal, like the conservative, wants to preserve the political, social, and economic institutions of the society. Unlike the conservative, however, the liberal has an ear attuned to any ideas and programs put forward by radicals and is willing to use these ideas and programs to conserve the society. The liberal and the conservative see the radical as a potential threat to the existing social order, but where the conservative prefers to put the radical out of circulation, the liberal tries to find a way to use him or make him harmless. Failing in both, the liberal joins the conservative to deal with the radical. Rather than actively joining the conservatives, however, the liberal simply disappears into silence, leaving the conservatives to deal with the radicals in whatever way may be necessary.

The political activities of this Presidential election year

were basically shaping up as a battle between the liberal and conservative forces in the country. The McCarthy and Kennedy challenge to Johnson was going to be a real fight until Lyndon Johnson removed himself as a candidate. Humphrey entered the race, but managed to keep himself out of the public arena. He wants to be the Democratic nominee and has gone to the smoky backrooms to get that nomination. By not campaigning in the primaries, he muted the sounds of the liberal-conservative battle within the Democratic Party and almost made McCarthy and Kennedy look like fools as they attempted to carry on campaigns against a phantom. Conservatism in the Democratic Party was embodied in Lyndon Johnson, but with Lyndon withdrawing from the fray and Hubert sneaking in and out of hotels, there was no target, nothing concrete for Kennedy and McCarthy to strike at.

On the Republican side, Richard Nixon was going about almost unnoticed, winning primaries by huge percentages and getting fantastic receptions wherever he went. His message was disarmingly simple and oh-so-good to the American ear—America is good. Americans are good. There is nothing wrong with the country. After eight years of massive social upheaval and a bewildering war, anybody who comes along and says a kind, reassuring word or two is bound to be popular. And for once Dick Nixon is popular. His only competition is coming from Rockefeller, whose political message seems to be, Gee, I'd sure like to be President.

Thus, as the Presidential nomination race was shaping up, there was only Bobby Kennedy waging a strong fight against a complete conservative takeover. McCarthy, despite his appeal to liberal youth, could only be regarded as a traitor to the liberal forces because he refused to drop out of the race and join forces with Bobby. He served to split a liberal camp that was not too strong to begin with.

Then came the assassination of Bobby, and if his death was not the result of a right-wing conspiracy, it is the right-wing which benefits most. Kennedy was the last buffer between the conservatives and their aspirations to take over the White House. Kennedy also stood as a buffer between the conservatives and the growing radical movement. In particular, he stood between the conservatives and the blacks. Kennedy recognized class differences within the black community and moved to exploit these. His tactic would have been to nullify whatever attempts would be made by black radicals toward disruption. The conservatives recognize one class—blacks—and as far as they are concerned, every black is untrustworthy. The conservative wants to make the entire black community pay for any act by a black radical group or individual. With Kennedy gone, the conservatives have nothing standing in their way.

Of course, it was clear before Kennedy died that he would not have gotten the nomination. Nonetheless, he would have remained a thorn in the side. The thorn now lies among the fallen rose petals.

None of this is to say that the attitude of radicals should have been any different toward Kennedy. Continued action by the radical movement would have forced him to the conservative position. The Indiana primary forced him to emphasize law and order over justice. In California he told white suburban audiences that McCarthy wanted to break up the ghetto and move the "hard-core unemployed" into suburbia.

For liberalism to be a viable force within this country,

it needed Bobby Kennedy. Without Kennedy, liberalism as any kind of significant political force is dead. McCarthy does not have the charisma to hold the liberal forces together. And if Ted Kennedy has any sense, he'll change his name to Radziwill and join the jet set.

It is clear at this point that conservatism will now begin to reign unchallenged in the country, and it doesn't matter whether Nixon or Humphrey gets into the White House. The radical movement has been spoiled in a sense, because it has flourished under conditions that were sometimes brutal, but never under conditions of total suppression. The black radical movement has existed under these conditions, but the white movement has had the protection of the Constitution to a great degree. That situation is going to come to an end. The arrest of Youth International Party leader Jerry Rubin in New York on June 13 for alleged narcotics possession is perhaps the first indication of this. The cops were much more interested in ripping Jerry's Fidel poster from the wall, in YIP's plans for Chicago, and in whom Jerry knew than they were in "pot."

If there is to be a wide radical movement within the country, now is the time to begin the formulation of new tactics and strategies. When the man is knocking at your door, it's too late. For us, Bobby Kennedy's death has much more political significance than his life ever did. That significance cannot be lost upon us if we intend to survive.

JUNE 22, 1968

# SIGNS OF REPRESSION

WHEN it comes, it comes quietly and almost invisibly. It is not announced on television or radio; there are no newspaper headlines or follow-up stories. When it comes, the mass media say that it has not come. When it comes, no one dares say that it has come. No one dares open his mouth and say what is obvious to all. Instead, people talk ever more loudly and ever more proudly about freedom, democracy, and peace. And a new soap powder is put on the market that promises even redder reds, whiter whites, and bluer blues, and my how those stars and those stripes will shine.

It is coming. Like a vine climbing the side of a building, it is coming. Each and every day. In New York, buses, cabs, and police cars are increasingly displaying decals of the American flag on their windshields. Neighborhood stores, barber shops, and bars display small flags in their windows. In Greenwich Village the owners of small arty shops report incidents where a small group of boys will come into the store, make snide remarks, sometimes threats, and then leave. The general intimidation of the presence of policemen is increasing in Greenwich Village, perhaps the area with the lowest crime rate in all of New York. In working-class neighborhoods the tension between whites and blacks is increasing. In one housing project in New York, white parents try to keep black children out of the project playground. In one incident, a white mother pulled a lead pipe out of her pocketbook to deal with an eight-year-old black child whom her son had pulled a knife on.

For eight years now, there has been protest in this country. The mass of Americans have been silent during this entire time. Yet one need not think that they have not been reacting to what has been transpiring. They are now beginning to make their reactions manifest. (Not in demonstrations, not by organizing political parties, not by petitions or ads in the papers. That is not the way the mass of Americans operate. In their lives, the overwhelming concern is making it from day to day, week to week, and month to month.) When they act, it is not in the national arena, but in the neighborhood and on the job. They recognize that there may be problems in the country, but that's okay as long as those problems don't reach the magnitude of threatening their own lives. The black movement, the antiwar movement, and the hippies are manifestations of problems within the society which have affected and threatened to disrupt the lives of every American. And when a man is threatened, he seeks to quiet that which is threatening him.

The left tends to view the police as instruments of the state. Undoubtedly they are, but it is more important to realize that they represent the attitudes and feelings of the mass of the people and act with their approval. A policeman is not some inhuman, sadistic ogre. He's a high-school graduate, with a wife and a couple of kids. He's buying a home and a car, and he's a cop because it's a good job and it gives him status in his community. Observe a cop in any neighborhood other than the minority or poor white communities. His relationship with small storeowners and people on the street is cordial and friendly. They like him. He is one of them. When the cops let right-wingers attack antiwar demonstrators, it is not necessarily because the cops may have right-wing views. In fact, the cops may disagree with both the right-wingers and the demonstrators. But during a historical period like this, the only politics that matters to a policeman (and the mass of Americans) is that which will stop whatever it is that is threatening the country's way of life.

Because the policeman is the uniformed representative of the majority community and has its support, everybody in that community is a potential policeman. The community itself does not become policeman until law and order break down to the extent that the uniformed policeman can no longer control it. When that happens, the police begin arming and training the community, as is happening now in such places as Detroit, Atlanta, Kansas City, and other cities across the country. When the community is ready to become policeman, it announces the fact by hanging flags in windows.

The American community (as opposed to the radical-hippie community) has been threatened and now feels a need to affirm itself, to reassert itself and its values. The long hair of the hippie is a threat only when it becomes so widespread that the parent in the American community looks at his child and sees a potential hippie. It becomes more than a generational gap. There has always been a generation gap in the West, but it was not serious as long as the child accepted the values of the parent. The gap existed only because the child wanted to do the same thing the parent did in his own way, and the parent was unable to see it. Now, however, the child not only does not want to follow the parent, he rejects everything the parent represents and considers good. It is no longer a generation gap; it is a conflict of cultures. When the child's rejection of the parent acquires a political content, then it is preordained that eventually the child must kill the parent or the parent the child.

At present, the parent is stronger and more organized. The child, still defenseless, can do but one thing—survive, grow stronger and stay ready. Above all, stay ready.

JUNE 29, 1968

## THE POOR PEOPLE'S CAMPAIGN AND RADICALS

THE Poor People's Campaign can be criticized for many reasons, and practically all of them would be correct. Yes, the Southern Christian Leadership Conference never had any intention of bringing about a real confrontation with the government. Yes, the poor were exploited and sold out, once again, by those who assigned themselves the job of acting in the name of the poor. Yes, the poor were brought to Washington, D.C., and put on exhibit, as it were, and after the nation had gotten an eyeful, the exhibit was unceremoniously taken down. But it is all too easy to criticize the campaign, and not much point in it, because what happened to the campaign was preordained, perhaps, when we as radicals refused to involve ourselves in it.

From the planning stage, the Poor People's Campaign was to be another demonstration extravaganza, produced and directed by black and white liberals. Possibly it was that which immediately turned a lot of us off. Perhaps it was that which made so many of us completely blind to the most fantastic accomplishment of the campaign. For the first time in the current era of protest activities, poor blacks, whites, Mexican-Americans, and Indians came together at the same place and the same time around their common condition.

It does not speak well of us that we did not formally involve ourselves in the campaign, that we did not show even the slightest interest in relating to what was happening and, more important, what could've happened in Washington. But perhaps this is another indication of the bourgeois bias and orientation of the radical movement. Or to put it differently, it is another indication of the fear that many of us have of poor people, of people from a different social background, of people who have to be related to on basic human terms and not on the level of radical rhetoric and theory and talk about relating to others on basic human terms. You can't intellectualize with the poor; you live with them. And maybe that is what frightens a lot of us.

The poor came to Washington and set up house between the Washington Monument and the Lincoln Memorial. That in itself was radical action. "The streets belong to the people," radical demonstrators in New York have yelled, and the erection of Resurrection City, even with government permission, was an act of saying that this country belongs to the people. The poor came to Washington and they were prepared to make themselves heard. The Indians shattered the majestic windows of the Supreme Court with a few soulful rocks. Over two hundred went to the Department of Agriculture cafeteria, ate, and left without paying. Food belongs to the people, also. Tijerina and the Mexican-

Americans were ready to take care of business. And everytime the poor tried to t.c.b., SCLC cut the ground out from under them.

At this point it can only be conjectured that things would've been different if the radical movement had involved itself. However, it seems probable, because the actions of the people themselves and the resultant suppression by SCLC of radical action indicates that if the people had been presented with leadership alternatives, the SCLC leadership would've found itself hurrying to keep up with the people, as it has been forced to do by the Student Nonviolent Coordinating Committee many times in the South.

From the time Martin Luther King announced plans for the Poor People's Campaign, it was obvious that the government was more up-tight than it had been in quite some time. With Dr. King's death and the subsequent burning and sacking of the nation's capital, the government was terrified of what could happen if the poor, en masse, came to town. The knife was poised above the government's throat, and we must share some of the guilt for allowing the government to take the knife from the hand and send everybody home coughing tear gas.

Perhaps we were turned off the Poor People's Campaign because we recognized that Congress would not respond to the demands being made. We, however, didn't recognize anything which the poor themselves did not recognize. The point of the campaign was to prove to all of the poor of America that the government didn't care, that there was no redress of grievances under the American system. And in an election year, that would've been a profound accomplishment.

But poverty is a condition that seems to be of concern

only to the poor and white missionaries when, in actuality, it is a *sine qua non* of revolution. There is no revolution until the potential for the existence of poverty has been destroyed. Poverty is, in the main, invisible in America, but its existence is no less real. America is increasingly fraught with the potential of more widespread and visible poverty. The increasing number of strikes is a testament to this. The American worker recognizes that his wages are increasing and he is getting power. And the only solution that he can now see is to strike for more money and more benefits. The Poor People's Campaign pointed feebly toward another solution—the country belongs to the people. By erecting a city on "federal property" and eating "free" at the Department of Agriculture, the poor were trying to dramatize this concept. The poor are constantly forced to accept the responsibility for their poverty, and when they move to act against those who are indeed responsible, it is the responsibility of all of us who consider ourselves radicals and revolutionaries to be with them. Our interests are one and the same.

The radical movement, however, lives too much with its eyes looking into its own brain. The poor were sold out in Washington, and by our absence and lack of concern, we have to share the responsibility for that sell-out. Congress acted as expected. SCLC acted as expected. And it is sad to think that, perhaps, we did, too.

JULY 6, 1968

## ON BEING REVOLUTIONARY

IT has been a year since the Newark rebellion, since last summer when in the midst of winter's sharpness we knew that the summer was going to be a long one, a hot one, one to be remembered always. This summer there is no mood of expectation, no anticipation of Armageddon. This summer no one knows what is going to happen next. There is only an uneasy waiting, and no one seems to know what to do or even where to look to find what to do. Things still happen, but they don't excite us. Last summer we all knew the ecstasy of the fires of Newark and Detroit, and in those fires there was some kind of hope. This summer we look and there are no such signs. If there are, we cannot see them or have not yet learned to read them.

When one is involved in revolution, it is all too easy to allow one's self to become discouraged. Particularly when one's revolutionary commitment is felt in intoxicating rhetoric, particularly when revolutionary fervor exists in the applause given a rousing speech, in the camaraderie of a demonstration or in the mind, where the ideal of revolution becomes a tool to work out personal problems for refugees from the bourgeoisie. Revolutionary commitment involves itself totally and completely with the destiny of humanity, and it is a commitment that is constantly tested, for there is no higher calling for any man than to be a revolutionary. The revolutionary acts, talks, and thinks differently than other men. He is different, for he carries within him the seed of the New Man. It is through the revolutionary that this New Man comes into being, and there is no greater responsibility than this.

The revolutionary must seize upon every experience as an opportunity to make himself more revolutionary, to make himself more the New Man. The revolutionary's commitment is not to the destruction of the dehumanizing system. His commitment is to the creation of the new system that will give birth to the New Man, and the destruction of the dehumanizing system is only a necessary prelude to the creation of conditions under which man may be fulfilled. Even as the revolutionary plans his attacks upon the dehumanizing system, even as he brings down the dehumanizing system, he keeps at the core of his Being, not the destroying, but the creating that must follow.

As we destroy, let us not forget that it is only so we may be more human.

As we destroy, let our exaltations not be for the blood that flows in the gutters, but for the blood that may more freely flow through our bodies.

We must destroy in order to live, but let us never enjoy the destroying more than the New Life, the only reason for the destroying.

If we forget, then those who come afterward will have

to destroy us for the Life that we, in our destroying, failed to give.

Revolution does not mean us against them. The revolutionary is a midwife seeking to give birth to the full potential of man. Involved in that most difficult of all births is our fighting against them, but let us not confuse that fight with Revolution.

In the psychosocial evolution of man, the revolutionary represents the final stage. Thus, one can never say that he is a revolutionary. One is only in a constant state of becoming revolutionary, of becoming more human.

It is an honor and a privilege to live now, to be one of those who accept the responsibility to kill the ideology of death and nurture the ideology of life. Yes, it is supremely difficult, but what of value is not.

So many of us have nothing more than a commitment to destruction, and that is not revolutionary. Others of us have a commitment to a certain way of analyzing, to a particular ideology, and do not understand that analysis and ideology are the tools of revolution and that strict adherence to that analysis and ideology does not automatically create revolutionaries or the revolution. And too many of us think that the sole function of revolution is to create institutions and life styles to help us overcome our own alienation. And how many of us got involved and when we realized what we had become involved in became frightened, for revolution requires a commitment so total that we have to dispense with all those dreams which we had held of what we wanted our lives to be?

Without any effort, tomorrow comes, but we can make that tomorrow what it should be and cease the inexorable procession of todays which feed upon humanity. We can do that if we understand the nature of revolutionary commitment and the nature of revolution. We can do that if we do not give way to despair when the traveling is difficult, or to arrogance when the way is easier.

The destiny of humanity rests with us. We should be honored to have been given such responsibility.

JULY 13, 1968

## WOMEN'S LIBERATION

SEVERAL years ago the question of women's liberation came up during a meeting of a radical black organization. The first person to speak was a prominent black male of the organization: "The position of the women in the movement should be prone!" That was the sum total of the discussion, and the meeting went on to "more important" matters.

Undoubtedly quite a few men in the movement would agree with that assessment as to the position of women. Fortunately, women don't agree. It is sad to think that any man who wishes to be considered radical, not to mention revolutionary, would not want for women what he wants for himself. Yet many men are finding the concepts of women's liberation groups and "liberated women" difficult to contend with. After all, within this society men comprise a privileged class, and the ideology which this society inculcates into us dictates that the man shall lead and the woman shall follow. That is all very well for an oppressive society, but for those of us who are (according to informed sources) trying to destroy the oppressive society and build the human one, it is unthinkable that men within the movement would fail to take seriously the necessity for women's liberation.

Of course, a privileged class is always unwilling to relinquish its privileges. It must be made to do so, and this is just what is beginning to happen with the formation of women's liberation groups around the country. Many men find the whole concept of women's liberation ludicrous, a matter to make jokes about and nothing more. Other men are forced to take it seriously when they are suddenly confronted with the children to feed while the wife goes to a meeting, when a girl friend suddenly isn't available twenty-four hours a day because she has to work on a poster or the organization's magazine. The usual male reaction is: What is it these women want? What're they talking about? That is a cop-out response, seeking to shift the responsibility of oppression to the oppressed. The reaction should be: What is wrong that has made it necessary for women to organize their own groups? And to answer the question, the man will have to look to himself and at the society.

This society forces male-female relationships into a cliché—man on top, woman on the bottom—and as long as the relationship remains in that cliché, the man feels comfortable and assumes the woman does, too. Once the woman seeks to change the position to side-by-side, the man tries to force her back to the bottom. He doesn't stop to think that maybe she's uncomfortable on her back. He just knows that he's more comfortable on top.

Within this society we grow up with the idea that a woman's reason for being is a man. Hollywood periodically presents us with a film about a woman being forced to choose between her man and her career, and inevitably, she chooses her man. The movie never suggests that even being presented with such a choice is false. A man doesn't have to choose either-or. Why, then, should a woman? Yet, America has created a category known as the "career woman." And the implication is clear that she's probably a lesbian, but would give up her career at a moment's notice for a "good man."

Not so strangely, it has always been men who have said that a woman's function in life was to serve a man. Now the women within the movement are talking to each other and seeking to define who they are, first in relationship to themselves. Any man who cannot see the beauty in this should question any claims he may make of being anything more than a liberal.

Many men treat the whole question of women's liberation lightly because they cannot see how it is politically relevant. They would prefer to defer the entire matter until that great day "after the revolution" and then, of course, women will automatically be liberated. Unfortunately it doesn't work that way. It is apparent that women cannot achieve liberation under the present system. None of us can. However, the present system will never be laid to rest unless the dynamics of personal relationships begin to change at the same time the present system is fought.

At present the movement tends to view women as necessary appendages. Women are no longer being considered as little more than an afterthought. The socialist revolutions of the 20th century have demonstrated that women are a vital necessity in the revolutionary struggle. The revolutionary potential of women cannot begin to be realized, however, as long as they are chained to this society's conception of what a girl friend, wife and mother should be. If the revolutionary potential of women is not realized, the revolutionary potential of men remains unrealized. As long as men accept this society's definition of women and male-female relationships, then men remain oppressed by this society. To the degree that a man views a woman as an object, he himself is an object. No man who is fully human can be threatened by women's liberation. Rather, he is overjoyed by it and realizes that women's liberation is also his responsibility.

JULY 20, 1968

## THE BATTLE OF CLEVELAND

JULY 23, 1968, will have to go down in the history of the black revolutionary struggle as a day of even more importance than July 25, 1967 (Detroit) and August 11, 1965 (Watts). It was on Tuesday night, July 23, that a small group of black men set up an ambush for the police in the streets of Cleveland, Ohio. They set it well and carefully: ". . . there were telephone complaints about an abandoned, stripped white Cadillac left on Beulah Street," wrote the *New York Post*'s Jimmy Breslin. "The police tow truck came up to the Cadillac, shots came from three directions. The driver was a civilian employe. He was not hit. He was doing what they wanted him to do, radio for help. They would use their aim later."

The police responded to the call for help, "and the first three cars pulled in and stopped. There was no shooting. The cops jumped out. Right away, heavy firing started . . . Louis Golonka sprang up and started running. Running in his black cop's shoes to make the corner, and he was in the middle of a stride when they got him and he went down on his face. Willard Wolff came away from the wall and ran toward Golonka. He was almost to Golonka and he was holding his hands out to grab for Golonka when he was hit and went down. He did not move. Leroy Jones, a lieutenant, came after the two of them and people were yelling at him, but Jones couldn't hear them in the noise and he was running when he was shot in the head and he fell on his face and died alongside a mailbox."

In fifteen minutes it was all over. Three cops were dead and fourteen wounded. Seven blacks died and one was wounded. Of those blacks killed, four were believed to have been guerrillas. The other three were fair game for the cops who killed them.

In military terms, it was a clear victory for the guerrillas. The police suffered seventeen casualties. The black community, seven. Mayor Carl Stokes quickly rounded up some of the best-known black nationalists in town. He was in trouble and had to arrest somebody in a hurry. One of the nationalists, Fred Ahmed Evans, claims that he was the organizer of the group that carried out the ambush. That may be. But then again, it may not. There was no political need for Evans to volunteer any information to the police. The deed had been done and it spoke eloquently for itself. Politically, it would've been wiser for Evans to yell "Frame-up!" But maybe the brother's on an ego trip.

Carl Stokes handled the over-all situation very well. His purpose for being in office was to keep "those people" in line, and in circumstances which would have sent a white mayor into a panic, Stokes showed that he could keep "those people" in line. Although he'd had the Governor call up the National Guard, he decided against immediately putting the Guard into the black community. Instead, he called together every Negro who had ever applied the name leader to himself and put upon them and the Negro policeman the responsibility of keeping the ghetto quiet. It was a gamble, and it worked to a greater degree that Stokes's white bosses had anticipated. Although there were some burnings and liberating of stores (looting) the night following the ambush, the people did not take to the streets as they would have had the Guard been in the community.

This ploy of Stokes is likely to be picked up rapidly by mayors from coast to coast. Instead of the colonial power using its own troops to police the native quarters, how much better it is to let the natives police themselves. And, it is a move which the ideology of the black movement has laid the ground work for. It is a move which takes advantage of the weaknesses of the "everybody-black-is-a-brother" position. It is a move which takes advantage of the calls for unity based on blackness rather than unity based on class and ideology. A black cop firing his gun at black people cannot be considered a brother. A black nationalist, a black minister, or a black political figure who walks the streets of the community and tells the people that fighting back is not the way is not a brother. A brother has one message and one message only—the best way to fight.

Under the guise of black unity, the black community is being divided. Under the guise of brotherhood and togetherness, one segment of the community is going to be used to police and oppress the other segment. And the ideological framework for this was laid by those who follow the Carmichael line—"Every Negro is a potential black man." How much more true is Rap Brown's statement—"Every Negro is a potential traitor. Every black man is a potential revolutionary."

It is to be hoped that the cadre which planned and carried out the ambush has also done its political homework and is carrying it into the community. In an urban situation, a guerrilla unit cannot survive unless it is simultaneously educating the people politically and thereby gaining their material support. The battle is not against cops. It is against a system which has created political and economic institutions whose sole aims are the oppression, degradation and exploitation of everyone. Cops are only an instrument of that system and have to be fought as long as they continue to be instruments. They are not the target, however. They are merely there to guard the target.

That there is a basis within the people for understanding the necessity and dynamics of revolution, there can be no doubt. The *New York Post* (July 24) reports an incident where the police were trying to chase some small boys off the street so they wouldn't get hit by any stray bullets from the guns of the guerrillas. One of the boys told the cops ". . . they're [the guerrillas] not after us. They're after you. They want you, not us." On that kind of understanding, a great and lasting revolutionary movement can be built, provided that we know what we want to build and what the necessary tools are for the building.

AUGUST 3, 1968

## BIRTH CONTROL AND BLACKS

IT is ironic to find the Pope's recent encyclical on birth control to be in line with the statements of many black militants. The Pope, of course, tries to place his opposition to birth control on moral grounds—that is, he argues that to prevent a life from coming into being is as much an act against moral law as willfully to take a life. Some black militants oppose birth control because they see it as a genocidal weapon against the black community, which, in those instances of forced sterilization of welfare mothers, it is. However, both the Pope and those militants who oppose birth control are giving allegiance in their own ways to an old principle: There is strength in numbers.

Of course, it would be ridiculous to expect that the most prestigious celibate in the world would have any understanding of the fact that to oppose birth control is to affirm woman control. The ideal woman to the Pope is an Ethel Kennedy, who seems to "drop one" every year. The Ethel Kennedys of the world can afford to give birth to ten a year, because they have the money to *not* raise their own children. Those black militants who stand up and tell women, "Produce black babies!", are telling black women to be slaves. If one could have eleven children and the Kennedy fortune, then by all means produce black babies. To have eleven children and a welfare check is almost akin to suicide, no matter how much black militants may want to romanticize the black mother. Undeniably, black mothers have done a fantastic job under incredible circumstances, but because black mothers have made a good showing of a bad thing, that doesn't mean it's desirable. Most often it is black males and women without children who are opposed to birth control. Neither group has much of a right to an opinion on the subject.

If blacks within the movement are seriously concerned about revolution, then they should be urging women to postpone having children, because women need to be free for the fullest participation in the struggle. It is no accident that in every revolutionary society, one of the first jobs is the setting up of birth-control clinics. Their aim is not to stop the birth of children for time immemorial. They recognize the very simple fact that most women want to have children. Their aim is merely to help a husband and wife plan when their children should come into the world, when it would be best for the parents and the society.

Most revolutionary countries go even further, and urge not only the postponing of families, but ask the youth to defer marriage until they reach their late twenties or early thirties. In Vietnam today there is a movement called "The Three Don'ts," which are: "If you meet a boy (girl), don't fall in love. If you fall in love, don't get engaged. If you get engaged, don't get married." If you are involved in a revolution, then the first necessity is to defer many of your personal desires. The first priority is the revolution.

Those black militants who oppose voluntary birth control are, in actuality, helping the enemy. As long as black women are confined to raising the family, the revolution will be without their necessary abilities. As long as they urge women to have children, they are confining women to be enslaved to their bodies, from which, with birth-control pills, they can now be so easily liberated.

The whole concept of birth control, as it is presented in this country, is a negative one, and perhaps it is this which many militants react against when they say, "Whitey is trying to tell you that you can't have black babies." It is not so much a matter of "controlling birth" as it is protecting the physical, mental, and spiritual health of women. To have a child is more than a physical act—much more. In actuality, giving birth to a child is a small part of the job and only the beginning. If one is a revolutionary, then he is concerned, above all, with the success of that revolution and all those involved. As long as we think that men are the only ones involved in revolution, we're bound to lose. As long as we insist on chaining women to their physiological beings, we lose.

The black woman may feel proud that the black man wants her to bear his children. She should feel proud, but if the black man sees birth control as a threat to his masculinity, then he should understand that no one wants to deny him his right to have a family. He is being asked to give his woman only the same opportunity to be a total revolutionary as he has been given by virtue of the fact that he is a man.

There is power in numbers, but that power is greatly

diminished if a lot of those numbers have to sit at home and change diapers instead of being on the front lines, where most of them would rather be.

AUGUST 17, 1968

## SNCC AND THE BLACK PANTHERS

AT its staff meeting in June, the Student Nonviolent Coordinating Committee reaffirmed its independence from the Black Panthers by voting not to adopt the Panther ten-point program as its own. It was thought that the Panther program was more reformist than revolutionary. This decision on SNCC's part did not help matters between the two groups, and everything came to a head within the past month at meetings held between representatives of the two groups. It is reported that the Panthers threatened SNCC leaders and at one point, several Panthers went for their guns. The shoot-out was averted, fortunately, but there was no doubt in the mind of any member of either organization that whatever merger or alliance may have existed was finished. One SNCC member stated bluntly: "I can't work with anybody I don't feel right turning my back on." All that was left at that point was for one of the organizations to inform the other that their formal relationship was terminated. SNCC took that step the first week in August.

At this point it seems doubtful that the two organizations will work out their differences in the near future. In an interview in the August issue of *The Movement,* Huey Newton had a long critique of SNCC in which he stated that SNCC had been controlled by white liberals until Stokely Carmichael's election as chairman. Anyone with any knowledge of SNCC history is aware that one of the unique features of the organization has been the fact that it has been controlled by blacks since its inception in 1960 and that whites were eventually expelled, not because they had too much power, but because they were ineffective working in the black community. Newton's analysis of SNCC's role in the black movement bore little relationship to the actual facts and further added to feelings within SNCC that the Panthers had never been interested in a real alliance or merger, but only in absorbing SNCC into the Panthers, and failing that, discrediting the organization.

That the two leading black radical organizations should regard each other with a suspicion and distrust that borders on hate really hurts. Perhaps the situation could have been avoided if SNCC had not allowed itself to be led into a relationship which it never really wanted. It is unthinkable that any organization would allow a few of its members to make a formal alliance with another group without anyone's approval. Yet this is essentially what happened.

Thus, a merger which never took place has been terminated. That would be fine if the "merger" had not taken place in public view and black and white radicals had not been deceived into believing that something existed which, in fact, didn't. It is incumbent upon any revolutionary organization to act with integrity and never to abuse the faith and hopes of the people. SNCC and the Panthers were acting in their own interests, and the people were forgotten. If anybody got hustled, it was not SNCC or the Panthers. It was Black America, which still waits for a revolutionary organization that will speak and act in its name.

When it became known this past spring that SNCC and the Black Panthers had "merged," the news was greeted with much excitement. It was the most logical move that could have been made to strengthen the black movement. SNCC was the one organization most responsible for the ideology of the black radical movement. The Panthers were the one organization working to concretize that ideology in the ghetto.

With the coming together of SNCC and the Panthers, the talk of black unity became more than talk. A merger between the two would have laid the basis for the creation of a national black radical organization at a time when the black community most needed it. Such a merger would have marked a new maturity on the part of the black movement. That "merger" existed, however, more in the minds of those who heard about it than anywhere else.

Earlier this month SNCC informed the Panthers that the SNCC central committee had voted to terminate the "merger" on the grounds that it had been made by individuals inside SNCC rather than the organization as a whole and that the exact nature and mechanics of the merger had never been fully discussed. (SNCC's Rap Brown and James Forman, who had been elected minister of justice and minister of foreign affairs of the Panthers, resigned from the Panthers. Stokely Carmichael, Panther prime minister, who was recently fired by SNCC, will probably work full-time for the Panthers now.) These were SNCC's official reasons for terminating the "merger," but these were mere technicalities. The actuality is that no functional merger between the two organizations ever existed and the possibility of there being one was remote from the beginning.

The first talk of any kind of merger began last winter when SNCC's James Forman returned from a visit to the San Francisco Bay area with the idea of an alliance between the Panthers and SNCC. People in SNCC were cool to the idea, because they knew very little about the Panthers. Stokely Carmichael had been drafted by the Panthers for one of their cabinet positions in 1967. There was some feeling in SNCC that the move to draft Carmichael should have come through the organization's central committee and not directly to Stokely, as Stokely was the spokesman for the organization, not only a public figure. Stokely and SNCC could not be separated, many in SNCC felt. Carmichael accepted the position with the Black Panthers. A few in SNCC felt this was a tactical error. The Panthers, then a young and virtually unknown organization nationally, might be trying to use Stokely to build themselves. SNCC, however, did nothing to prevent Carmichael from joining the Panthers.

SNCC, which has always lacked the ability to discipline its members, did nothing, either, to stop Forman from making an alliance with the Panthers. The formal announcement of the alliance was to have been done officially at a Free Huey Rally on February 17 of this year in Oakland. Forman, Carmichael, and Rap Brown were to be present, as well as the Panther hierarchy. However, Eldridge Cleaver, Panther minister of information, broke the news on February 11 at a Peace and Freedom Party forum at which he made observations about SNCC which did little to improve the "merger" prospects. In that speech, published in the March 16 issue of the Panther newspaper, Cleaver stated: "What we have done is worked out a merger with SNCC. The Black Panther Party for Self Defense and SNCC are going to merge into a functional organization. . . ." This was news to SNCC.

The organization was under the impression that it was entering into only an alliance with the Panthers, which to most in SNCC was little more than good public relations. The "merger" was something SNCC first learned of when word of Cleaver's speech reached them. SNCC sought to clear the matter up, and Cleaver is reported to have said that what he meant by "merger" was alliance. Yet at that Free Huey Rally in Oakland on February 17, he repeated that a "merger" had been made and continued to speak thereafter of the relationship between the two organizations as a "merger."

Cleaver further jeopardized SNCC-Panther relations when he stated in that same February 11 speech that, "It is very important to realize that SNCC is composed virtually of black hippies . . . of black college students who have dropped out of the black middle class . . ." Possibly he meant it as a joke, but SNCC did not find it funny. It was not only a put-down of SNCC, but of black college students as well. The fact that he would so describe SNCC was questionable, and to do so before a white audience did not endear him or the Panthers to SNCC.

Cleaver continued his speech to imply strongly that the ideology which SNCC's spokesmen, Stokely and Rap, preached, had, in actuality come from the Panthers: "Most people don't know this, but a lot of the rhetoric you hear from Stokely Carmichael and Rap Brown these days . . .

was adopted precisely because they had come to the West Coast and spent a little time with the Black Panthers out here . . ."

It was remarks such as these that fed the suspicions of many in SNCC that the organization was being "hustled" by the Panthers. Whether or not this is true cannot, of course, be ascertained. Yet the question was asked by many in SNCC that if Cleaver and the Panthers thought so little of SNCC as publicly to call them "black hippies," why then would they want to "merge" with them? In his February 11 speech Cleaver gave an answer: ". . . what they [SNCC] have done is made their apparatus available to us and there's no hangup; we can move into that." Many in SNCC felt that that "apparatus" was having the names Carmichael, Forman, and Rap officially associated with the Panthers.

Many Panthers were also suspicious of the "merger." They viewed SNCC as a dying organization which was simply trying to exploit the Panthers to keep alive. Undoubtedly, SNCC was having serious internal problems, but SNCC did not see a "merger" with the Panthers as the solution. With each organization questioning the other's motives, suspicion and distrust merged in both groups before any other kind of merger had a chance.

August 24, 1968

## YIPPIES IN CHICAGO

THEY are constantly held up to ridicule and scorn; they are the subjects of cartoons, the butts of jokes, raw data for sociological analysis. With their long hair, it is occasionally difficult to distinguish male from female. Their clothes are disheveled and sometimes dirty. Their talk is often extravagant, enthusiastic, and nonrational. They pay an allegiance to drugs and music that is only slightly less than that of a devout Catholic to the Pope. They are praised by no one except themselves and yet they persist in their own determination to define and determine their lives for themselves despite the disapproval of society and the condemnation of their parents.

Yet when one sees them strolling down Chicago's swank Michigan Avenue and gathering outside the Conrad Hilton Hotel to protest at the arrival of Senator Eugene McCarthy, there is something very beautiful about them. When one sees them wandering in the midst of the red-white-and-bluehatted McCarthy-McGovern-Humphrey boys and girls, there is something beautiful and real about them.

It is difficult to believe what is called America until one looks at the faces of the delegates to the Democratic convention. It is difficult to believe that faces such as these exist—fat, smooth, cornflake-fed faces which cannot imagine the world that exists beyond the fields and small-town front yards where cornflakes grow. It is difficult to believe the thin, cosmetic-choked tight faces of the women, who gave birth to their children in screaming pain and then proceeded to revenge themselves upon their children. This is America, and one cannot imagine the beauty of revolution dawning within these souls. These are faces for which law and order are synonymous with justice. These are faces which become red with pride at the sight of a flag. These are the faces which the young ones, the long-haired ones, grew up with, looked into for the hope which is necessary to grow, and decided, Hell, No! We Won't Go the road you have gone.

They have repudiated the Americans who later this week will be screaming and cheering at the sight of balloons dropping from a ceiling, who will be marching and yelling and waving placards, wearing ridiculous hats, and with great solemnity and seriousness of purpose, nominating a man for President. They have repudiated the values their parents and their country have offered them, and they are the only examples of white humanity seen to date in this garrisoned city.

Smug, self-righteous new left ideologues limply put down the yippies for being politically immature and irresponsible. Those of us who involve ourselves in more overt political action have no guarantee to the truth, but because we are trying to follow in the footsteps of Lenin, Mao and Fidel, we arrogantly think we do. This is America. Not Russia, China, or Cuba, and in America, maybe, just maybe, the paths to revolution will be clothed not only in guerrilla uniforms but beads and incense.

Yippies will soon fade from the American cultural revolution, having done their job of politicizing thousands who could not be politicized through facts, figures, or theories. The American ideology of revolution is evolving, and the yippies' contribution to that has not been small. It is the new left ideologue who stands to lose by snobbishly ignoring the yippies, not the reverse.

August 31, 1968

# THE CHICAGO DEMONSTRATIONS

ALL year everyone looked forward to Chicago. Some with anticipation. Some with dread. Chicago was to be the major confrontation of the year. Some on the left were afraid that McCarthy—and before his death, Kennedy—would co-opt the antiwar forces in Chicago. For that reason, they advocated not going to Chicago. Others advocated not going because it was going to be a massacre. But arguments against Chicago meant very little. A confrontation was going to take place there whether anyone wanted it or not.

The confrontation has now taken place. It did not involve the hundreds of thousands which had been predicated. Most who had thought about going to Chicago were sufficiently intimidated and frightened by the well-publicized military preparations made to insure "domestic tranquillity." So instead of 100,000 demonstrators, no more than 10,000 came, but that was sufficient. If 100,000 had come, Chicago would now be on the bottom of Lake Michigan. And when one recognizes that there were no more than 10,000 or so demonstrators in the streets of Chicago, it is a testimony to the strength of a committed minority.

The demonstrations are also a testimony to the impact that nonviolent demonstrations can have. And anyone who criticizes the demonstrations for being nonviolent is being foolishly romantic. The easiest thing to have done in Chicago would've been to commit suicide—and large, Paris-style demonstrations would've been just that. The military might on display in Chicago dictated nonviolent demonstrations if a massacre was to be averted. There were, however, some acts of violence on the part of demonstrators which showed that the spirit of resistance and retaliation was very much present. The Conrad Hilton Hotel was filled for three consecutive nights with the stench of stink bombs. Police cars were destroyed. A small number of cops were injured. But these were acts of individuals separated from the mass and not acts of the mass, as in ghetto rebellions. Thus, the mass was spared the full brutality of the military.

In many respects the Chicago demonstrations were reminiscent of the demonstrations of the civil rights movement. Do something and let the government's forces react to you. For this tactic to be successful, one must have a thorough knowledge of the enemy, a knowledge so thorough that what you do is "program" him. This happened in Chicago. And all it requires is a willingness to be gassed, beaten, and even killed. Or, to put it differently, it requires a commitment so strong that being gassed, beaten, or killed isn't that frightening a prospect.

In Chicago, the enemy was programed into using massive brutality at the time when it was most detrimental to him. Not only were the demonstrators victims of this brutality, but the liberal establishment itself was attacked. Not once, but repeatedly, the press was attacked—and the reason was stated very directly by one policeman, who screamed at a news photographer, "Why don't you take a picture of them throwing rocks?"

That was it. The resentment and anger finally burst out. For four years now the police have been under constant attack from blacks, from demands for civilian review boards, from the liberal establishment. In Chicago, the police retaliated. They drew that line between the good guys and the bad guys a little tighter, and the only qualification for being a good guy was that you thought the cops were good guys. Liberals were pushed into the same camp with leftists, yippies, hippies, and blacks. It is no small matter when cops will beat people in the lobby of the Conrad Hilton Hotel, when they will push well-dressed spectators through plate glass windows, when they will go into McCarthy campaign headquarters and pull kids out of bed and beat them.

And the liberal establishment recognized what happened. It was no longer a matter of antiwar demonstrators being attacked. It was "our children" who were being attacked. And Tom Wicker in the September 1 *New York Times* was quick to point out that "These were not Negroes, rioting and burning in the ghetto; there were few black faces among the demonstrators. These were not snipers, looters, or terrorists. No mobs were clashing with one another. No plastic bombs or Molotov cocktails were thrown . . . The truth is that these were our children in the streets, and the Chicago police beat them up." And if the children were being attacked, so were the parents. That was the inescapable conclusion the liberal establishment had to make.

The demonstrations forced liberals to confront as never before the question of how much they can continue to work within the system. Most will undoubtedly work all the harder to prove to themselves and the young that the system can work. But a minority will return to their communities and ask questions they hadn't asked before of those around them. Just what answers they produce will depend in part on whether or not radicals will avail themselves of this opportunity to move a few more people to a more radical political outlook. The opportunity is present and it must be taken advantage of.

SEPTEMBER 7, 1968

## GEORGE WALLACE AND THE PEOPLE

IN his acceptance speech at the Republican convention, Richard Nixon called them "the forgotten Americans." He wasn't referring to the Indians, the people to whom the phrase is usually applied. ("Ignored" would be a more apt phrase for them.) He was speaking of the vast majority of middle- and lower-middle-class white Americans who have not been "forgotten" so much as they've been taken for granted during the past eight years. They could be taken for granted by the politicians, however, because they were either Repulicans or Democrats, and when elections rolled around, they could be depended upon to vote as their traditional loyalties dictated.

This year Presidential nominees of both parties are outdoing each other for the votes of this large group because one man did not take them for granted. George Wallace, a man few ever took seriously until recently, has been traveling around the country speaking to these Americans and being received as a "comrade" by them.

His message is disarmingly simple: You are somebody. George Wallace recognized that these "forgotten Americans" were perhaps more alienated from the society than the children of affluence, the children of the ghetto, and the liberal intellectual. They were more alientated because they were without a means of even expressing their alienation. They looked at the world about them, a world of rapid and cataclysmic change, and saw that change as only a threat. And they could find no political force that could speak to their fears and quiet them or speak to their fears and organize them. No one came forward to move them into the process of change, so their fears increased. George C. Wallace has come forward to articulate those fears and organize them. George Wallace is saying publicly what many whites have been saying to themselves and each other. He is reenforcing their resistance to change and cannot be glibly written off as a fascist and a demagogue. George Wallace is real, and the people for whom he speaks are the people whom we see every day but never speak to. And perhaps that is why they are so receptive to George Wallace now.

"I think there is a backlash in this country," Wallace says, "against the theoreticians—some of them in some of our colleges and some of our courts and some of our newspaper editors' offices and some of our pulpits—who look down their nose at the steelworker and the paper worker and the communications worker and the beautician and the barber and the policeman and the fireman and the little business man and the clerk and the farmer and say that you don't have intelligence enough to decide how to get up in the morning and when to go to bed at night, and people are tired of theorists running their country."

Wallace is angry at what has been done to his cherished

beliefs, like the cops in Chicago were angry when the demonstrators would sing "My Country 'Tis of Thee," like the cops in Brooklyn are angry at the very existence of an organization of blacks called the Black Panthers. Wallace and his constituents also share with us the frustration of a system which increasingly allows for less and less involvement in anything remotely human. The significant difference is that we find the fault in the system; Wallace finds no fault in the system, but fault only in some segments of the populace who are impeding the system's working to its best advantage. Wallace's appeal is essentially emotional. The practically unaninous support he enjoys among white policemen throughout the country is based solely on the fact that in his speeches he always calls for a round of applause for "our fine policemen." In his emotional appeal lies his main strength, for his political solutions will bring us to the brink of civil war faster than anything else could. Of course, a civil war would not sadden most of Wallace's constituency since it figures that it has the necessary strength on its side. And it is safe to say that it does.

Everyone is trying to calculate just what effect Wallace is going to have on the Presidential race. It is amusing to see Humphrey and Nixon trying to co-opt Wallace with very little chance of success. Most predictions say that Wallace is going to take the Republican vote from Nixon, but recent political history refutes that. When John Lindsay ran for Mayor of New York City, his opponents were Democrat Abraham Beame and Conservative William Buckley. The predictions were that Buckley would hurt Lindsay and help elect Beame. As it turned out, Buckley cut into the labor and lower-middle-class vote, which was traditionally Democratic, and thereby gave Lindsay the edge. It is safe to say that Wallace will help Nixon to the White House, since Wallace's strength outside the South is in the area of labor and the lower middle class. It is these people who have felt the brunt of the black revolution and the revolt of the children of affluence.

Wallace is accomplishing what Gene McCarthy could not. Wallace has gone to the people, and the people have put him on the ballot in practically every state. He has built his own party, his own organization, and has created a viable alternative to the Republican and Democratic parties, which refused to create much distinction between each other.

And Wallace has unmistakably shown us whom we need to reach. They are alienated. We are alienated. We see a long-range solution that will benefit all. Wallace offers them an emotional palliative and a solution of "jail those of your enemies you can't kill." The question for us is not how can we reach those whom Wallace has reached. Forget them. They are lost. We must reach their sons and daughters, our contemporaries who work behind the pizza counters, at the drive-ins, who are apprentices in the unions with their fathers. They are the future, and we must reach them at the level of their need before George Wallace does.

SEPTEMBER 14, 1968

# THE RUSSIAN OCCUPATION OF CZECHOSLOVAKIA

MANY radicals were disturbed and confused by the Russian invasion of Czechoslovakia. Almost all felt that they had to choose who was right and who was wrong in this context, and the Czechs won. Their freedom had been trampled by mean ol' Russia. And everyone wept a few sentimental liberal tears for occupied Prague.

This kind of reaction to the recent events in Eastern Europe is more a reflection of our youth and untested idealism than it is a reflection of whatever might have occurred there. What would have been our reaction if Fidel had had to send troops onto the campus of the University of Havana to put down a student uprising which threatened the evolution of socialism in Cuba? What would have been our reaction to Ho Chi Minh's unhesitating elimination of thousands of political foes in the mid-1950's if we had been politically active then? And our reaction is decidedly negative to the purges under Stalin, even though we know nothing about them.

This will undoubtedly be interpreted by some as a covert approval of Russian action against Czechoslovakia. It is not. Nor is it disapproval. Perhaps the correct position on the matter was that taken by China and Cuba—condemnation of both Russia and Czechoslovakia. Neither country is a model of socialism that anyone is following, and serious questions can be raised as to whether either country is totally worthy to be called socialist. But all of that is irrelevant to our infant movement's taking sides because we see pictures of tanks entering a city and, like well-conditioned animals, we scream that he at whom the tank is aimed has been wronged. This kind of reaction reveals an all too typical American syndrome— apolitical morality.

It was most distressing to see the many signs during the demonstrations in Chicago equating Chicago with Prague. "Welcome to Prague" and "Chicago Is Prague" were the most common. Why did the students have to go halfway around the world to find a people to identify with? Had they forgotten the National Guard in Newark, the Army in Detroit, and the police in every black community around the country? Had they forgotten that the Army was camped in the black community of Chicago at the very time they were demonstrating?

Black suspicion of white radicals is well known by now, and one of the problems which many white radicals have concerned themselves with is how to overcome this suspicion. That suspicion cannot be overcome as long as white radicals can equate Chicago with Prague, as long as the black deaths of Watts, Detroit, Newark, and everywhere else in this country fail to hurt inside whites as painfully and continually as they hurt inside blacks. For all that was good about the Chicago demonstrations, more concern was shown for the Vietnamese than for blacks. The war in Vietnam was the rallying point, not the war on black America. Rap Brown is still a political prisoner. Huey Newton is still in jail. Lee Otis Johnson, a worker for the Student Nonviolent Coordinating Committee in Texas, has been sentenced to thirty years in jail. The Black Panthers in New York are under constant attack. Yet white radicals find it easier, in many places, to link their movements to Vietnam and Prague. Yes, what happens in Vietnam and even Prague affects the movement here, but it is here and not there that our movement will either win or be crushed.

Chicago is not Prague. Chicago is Chicago, and any attempt to make Chicago analagous to Prague is only evading a crucial question of our movement. How can the children of the colonial power disarm the suspicion of the children of the colony? The question cannot be answered by the white radical government's mechanically taking orders from the black movement, but only by radical action which has as its focus the resolution of the problem: liberty or death. And it is only when a movement's attention is focused on this that the revolutionary struggle has begun.

SEPTEMBER 28, 1968

# THE DECEPTION OF RHETORIC

SOMETIMES we are the victims of our own words. At best, words are poor conveyors of information. They are imprecise and must be used with the utmost care if they are to do what we want them to do. When they are used imprecisely, improperly, and without regard for the many dangers inherent in them, they can turn upon the the user, confounding and confusing him, and eventually be the cause of the user's destruction.

We of the left are in danger of falling victim to our own words. We have proclaimed to one and all that we are revolutionaries and involved in revolution. We have proclaimed that the revolution has begun, and if red flags are a sign of revolution, then indeed it has. All of us use this word "revolution" like a manufacturer making certain that the name of his product gets in every sentence of a commercial. And because it makes us feel good to be revolutionaries involved in revolution, we fail to ask ourselves if we are, indeed, involved in revolution, if we are, indeed, revolutionaries.

To a limited degree, it is clear that we are involved in a revolution. A revolution, however, is not *the* revolution, and too many of us mistake the former for the latter. The revolution we are presently involved in is a cultural one, an uprising of the young against the values which the society is based upon and perpetuates. It is a revolution which has involved an explosive and painful groping for new life styles, new mores, new music, new uses of the mass means of communication. It is a revolution which has seen the young go into the streets to confront the present with the new of their uncut hair, the new of their multicolored clothes, covering less and less of their bodies (which are real and good and beautiful and yes, yes it is nice to touch each other, isn't it?). They have been willing to accept the consequences of their new life styles of lying on the grass openly passing "joints," of saying no to the government's immoral demand for two years of your life in a uniform to fight a war, of repeatedly placing their bodies in the streets.

It has been a cultural revolution, but not a political revolution. It has been a cultural revolution with political consequences, political ramifications, political meaning, because culture and politics cannot be separated. It has been a middle-class cultural revolution, bearing no similarity to the cultural revolution in China, which was named with scientific precision, the Proletarian Cultural Revolution. The proletariat have been the spectators of our revolution, eagerly reading the newspaper and magazine articles about us, but still regarding us as different from them.

It has been a cultural revolution which has brought

an ever-growing consciousness of the necessity for a revolution which changes the economic structure of the country, because all of the cultural, social and political institutions of the country evolved to justify and maintain the economic structure. While our revolution has threatened the nation's sense of psychological security, the economic structure remains intact, leisurely chewing up millions of people every day.

We defeat ourselves by calling what we have brought about "revolution." It is a step toward that revolution, but we have not begun to approach that day when we have seized power, held it and begun to create a system that is based on a sense of community (which does not mean living together physically). When we call what we have done thus far revolution, we give ourselves the feeling that we have done much more than we actually have. We blind ourselves to the difficulties in front of us. We blind ourselves to the dangers on every side.

The feeling that revolution is a necessity is the mere beginning and is really nothing to compliment oneself for feeling. Anyone who is not afraid to feel his humanity feels the necessity for the creation of a society in which man can truly be man and woman can truly be woman. The implementation of that revolution is a job requiring a scientific precision. The tide did not stop because King Canute yelled at it. This system will not disappear because we say "fuck the system," or because we know all the right things to say. This system will die only if we do everything from having a correct analysis to getting shoelaces for the guerrillas who will one day be fighting. This system is highly organized, and to be certain that it is maintained, the caretakers of the system attend to every detail, even to the extent of trying to anticipate what details will need attending to in fifty years. We say that we are involved in a revolution because we feel better about ourselves. A revolutionary, however, does not exist for himself. In fact, it is his own self which exists least for him, because at the same time that he feels revolutionized within, he feels the pain of the selves that have not been revolutionized. And as long as one man is enslaved, all of us are enslaved. Thus, Che Guevara, who could've rested on his laurels, went to Bolivia.

The revolution is not yet. The seeds have been planted, but whether those seeds will receive the sunlight, water, and proper cultivation which they desperately need depends upon our ability to look honestly at ourselves and recognize that the time has come when it is suicidal self-indulgence to engage in romantic role-playing. When this system is threatened, it bares its teeth and claws and fights and cares not who sees. (The networks photographed the beatings of Chicago in color.) The system plays for keeps. It will destroy us or we will destroy it. It is that simple. As Rap Brown says, "In revolution one either walks off the battlefield victorious or is left lying there." At least, if we are left lying there, let it not be because we committed suicide.

October 5, 1968

# THE LIMITS OF THE STUDENT MOVEMENT

A STUDENT movement has its own built-in limitations, both in terms of how much it can do and how much it can understand. In some ways, a student movement tends to be artificial, because the student lives in an artificial environment—the university. Thus, it is natural that a student movement generally concerns itself with issues that the majority of society has hardly any time at all to be concerned about. This is good to a point. Without the student demonstrations against the war, there would've been no antiwar movement. Without student consciousness of racism, blacks would be even more isolated and vulnerable to attack.

A student movement evolves to an inevitable point where it realizes that wars and racism are the manifestations of an inhuman system, and if wars and racism are going to be stopped, the system itself must be stopped and another created. And it is at this point that a student movement reaches the boundaries of its inherent limitations. When this juncture is reached, the student movement finds its members becoming increasingly frustrated and the movement seeks to relieve that frustration through activism and/or by turning its attention to changing the students' immediate environment, the university.

A student movement which concerns itself with bringing about changes within the university is engaging in an act which can have all the appearances of being important, while being, in essence, quite unimportant. Regardless of how unending one's stay in a university may seem, the fact yet remains that after four years of serving time, the student leaves. The university is a temporary society for most who live within its confines, and as such, any radical activity aimed at it is of limited value.

Because the university is a temporary society, any movement coming from it is in danger of being temporary. The next student generation may have more traditional interests than the one which kept the campus in an uproar during the preceding four years. And while student movements are characterized by a great willingness to confront the reigning social authority, there is nothing inherent in a student movement that will insure its evolution into a radical movement once the students leave the university.

Perhaps the greatest liability of a student movement is that it is able to speak only to other students. While this is of limited value, the fact still remains that there is perhaps no group more powerless than students. Not only are students without power, the instruments of power are not even a part of their world. If all students went on strike, it wouldn't cause the society to pause in its step. The most that a student movement can do is to disrupt. The power to disrupt, however, cannot be equated with the power to make a revolution. A student movement is a revolutionary force only when it can act as an adjunct with other forces in the society. It is needless to say that such a situation does not presently exist.

When student radicals leave the campus, they can avoid coming into direct contact with other forces in the society by creating their own little worlds where they continue to live with each other, talk only to each other and remain unconcerned about the concrete problems which most people have to face. The student radical is never heard talking about a rise in the price of milk, new taxes, real wages or doctor's bills. The student radical creates his own society in which money is not an overriding problem and because it isn't, the student radical thinks that revolution is all about love, because he has time to think about love. Everybody else is thinking about survival.

No matter how radical a student may be, his radicalism remains virgin until he has had to face the basic problems which everyone in the society has to face—paying the rent every month. It is easy to be radical when someone else is underwriting it. It is all too easy to belittle the Wallace-supporting factory worker when one does not know the constant economic insecurity and fear under which that factory worker lives.

While the goal of revolution is the creation of the New Man, people turn to revolution when that becomes the only means of satisfying their material needs. They do not become revolutionaries because of any ideas about the New Man.

The student radical has to become an everyday radical before he can be totally trusted. He must know the concrete problems which face the everyday person. And while such issues as the war in Vietnam, the repression of Mexican students, and the invasion of Czechoslovakia are important, revolution is made from the three eternal issues—food, clothing, and shelter. The American system requires of its people that they exchange their lives and humanity for food, clothing, and shelter. Our job is to show people that they are being robbed of their birthright for a mess of pottage and that that is not necessary.

As long as the movement is dominated by students, the movement will carry within it the seeds of its own death. As long as the student, upon graduation, carries his radicalism to an apartment three blocks away from the campus or to the nation's East Villages where a thousand others just like him reside, his radicalism will remain theoretically correct and pragmatically irrelevant, except as a gadfly forcing the system to make minimal reforms.

October 26, 1968

# THE FAITH OF THE REVOLUTIONARY

WE look at them, their fat, sagging bellies, hard faces, tight lips, and we despair. It is logical in our eyes that they should support Wallace, for they are ugly and Wallace is ugly and we are beautiful and gentle and want to do nothing more than love everyone in the rising of each sun. We look at them, and the conclusion is quickly reached that they will never change. They will always be filled with resentments, fears, and hates. And having so concluded, we end our examination and analysis of them and prepare to wait for more propitious times.

It is difficult to be a revolutionary, for to be a revolutionary means to believe in the innate goodness of man and to know that man in this environment has been programed into nonman. Our job is to change the environment so that man can be man.

It is particularly difficult to be a revolutionary at a time when man's capacity for infinite evil is being unleashed. But the job yet remains to look into those faces and to remember that they do not have control of their lives, either. They are the victims, also, and must be made to realize it. Perhaps that is not a task we can do. Well paid, well fed, well housed and clothed victims are quite often willing to accept their state as long as they are well rewarded. But even if they are as yet unable to recognize their condition, we must not forget what it is. Even if we have to regard them as the enemy, we must not forget that they, too, are victims.

All too often, though, we confuse the doer with the deed and think that they are one and the same. It is the deed we must hate, not the doer of the deed. The policeman acts like a beast, but to call him a beast, a "pig," is only to negate the potential of man that is within him. We must learn that attitude which is exemplified in Cuba and North Vietnam, where any person you meet will say, "We do not hate the American people. The people are our friends. We hate the American government." The Vietnamese and Cuban people welcome Americans to their country, while the one country is fighting for its life against America and the other exists under the constant threat of annihilation. To yell "Fascist!" at a Wallace supporter is only to guarantee that that individual will be a fascist.

None of us were born revolutionaries. Therefore, if we have found within ourselves the capacity to change, we must acknowledge that everyone else has the capacity to change. Once we acknowledge this, we must then begin to live and act as if we believe it. The Cuban rebel army would attend to the wounded enemy soldiers after each battle, for Fidel recognized that the man he had just shot could be a revolutionary. And imagine the shock of the wounded soldier as he had his wounds bandaged by those whom he had just been trying to kill. What manner of men were these? They were revolutionaries. The New Man.

People will be changed as much by our words as by our actions. Mao's Red Army converted many peasants to their side because this was an army that did not come into a village and steal the crops and rape the women. It paid the peasant for whatever food was taken and respected each and every peasant. The men in the Red Army were different from the men in the uniform of the Kuomintang, and it was because they were different that the fears of the peasant were destroyed.

Because the style of our movement has been determined by our need to work out our own problems, we do not know how to reach those who are different from us. We have repudiated their life styles, but if we are going to reach them, it may be necessary for us to adopt that style which is so repugnant to us. For us, male and female, profanity is the natural punctuation in a sentence. For them, profanity is used in certain social settings and never in front of women. For us a church is a building that people go to on Sunday because they haven't learned the value of sleeping late. For them church is an integral part of life, and he who does not attend church is ostracized by the community. When the Student Nonviolent Coordinating Committee was organizing in the South, there was never any doubt in the organizer's mind that he would go to church on Sunday morning. He had to if he expected the people in the community to listen to anything he had to say. Yet there were white kids who came South and wanted to argue the existence of God with the local people.

Perhaps it is time for some of us to go back home, to remind ourselves that everything there was not bad. One of the basic problems which has faced many white activists is the fact that they hate the white community. Undoubtedly the feeling is to some degree justified. Yet there is work to be done there. It won't be as easy as lying around somebody's apartment in a big city, smoking pot and thinking up slogans for the next demonstration. In fact, it's a lifetime job requiring total commitment. But if that revolution is going to be born, the work must begin.

Yes, they are ugly. Their faces are filled with spite and hate. But did they deliberately sit in front of the mirror and create those faces? Or were they forced to live lives which tightened the flesh of their faces into a perverted contortion of humanity?

"One must have faith in the best in men," José Martí wrote, "and distrust the worst. If not, the worst prevails."

We must acquire that faith.

NOVEMBER 2, 1968

## THE MEDIA AND THE CULT OF THE PERSONALITY

SOMETIMES it seems that history does, indeed, repeat itself. The mistakes of a radical movement are sometimes repeated several generations later by another radical movement. At other times a radical movement will repeat its own mistakes within the same generation. Mistakes are, of course, inevitable. They are not bad in and of themselves if the factors which caused the mistakes are recognized and corrected. Ignorance is our greatest enemy. To know what to do, when to do it and why it is being done is the preeminent task at all times. When mistakes are repeated, it is an indication that there is a serious, perhaps fatal, lack of revolutionary consciousness.

Since the enunciation of Black Power in 1966, the black radical movement has shown itself to be overly media-oriented. In the early spring of 1966 the media turned their blinding glare on blacks and on Stokely Carmichael in particular. He became the medium through which the feelings of young blacks were articulated. And because of the ever-present television cameras and newspaper reporters, he became more than an instrument of black people. He became an entity in his own right, a public figure, a world personality. If one does not have a fully developed revolutionary consciousness and commitment, this kind of public attention can be dangerous. The human ego is like an insatiable tick. If it is not killed, it can burrow under the layers of the soul and feed upon the man within, gorging itself until there is no man left.

To become a public personality in Western society is to become a prisoner of a media-created image. To become a public personality in a revolutionary society is to become so at one with the people that quite unconsciously they see you in them and you see yourself in them. The West says a "cult of the personality" exists in the figures of Mao and Fidel. That is not true. Revolutionary consciousness and revolutionary commitment have destroyed the ego in Mao and Fidel, and in that destruction, they as men became free. Mao is China. Fidel is Cuba. China is Mao. Cuba is Fidel.

In this society that kind of total submersion of the person into the people and vice versa is almost impossible if one does not cut himself off from everything except the people. Carmichael's leadership position came not from this kind of total submersion, but from his rhetoric and aggressive image on which the media voraciously gorged itself. Slowly, the rhetoric and the aggressive image began to devour the Student Nonviolent Coordinating Committee and Carmichael. The rhetoric replaced program. The image replaced organizing. Sometimes it even seemed that Carmichael would say whatever was necessary to get the desired response, instead of saying whatever was necessary to build revolutionary consciousness. Words are a revolutionary tool only when they are used toward revolutionary ends. Words must eventually be made manifest in a revolutionary program, organizing and action. That did not happen.

For a year now Carmichael has not used the media to address himself to black people. Partially that was through choice and partially it was because others had come forward to play the same role Carmichael had. With their black berets and black leather jackets, the Black Panthers present a striking image. With their rhetoric of power made manifest with the gun, it is not surprising that their Neilsen rating would be a little higher than Carmichael's. Add to this an official of the organization whose credentials are that of being an ex-convict-rapist-revolutionary who can write, and you face a situation so fraught with dangers that the mind shudders to contemplate them.

From the time of their demonstration in the California State Capitol, it was evident that the Panthers (at least on the West Coast) were media-oriented. But one cannot seriously organize a revolutionary movement in the glare of publicity. While the media can help an organization get its message through to hundreds of thousands of people more quickly than could be done in any other way, the media also alert the enemy before you may be in a position to deal with him. The enemy did not hesitate to move against the Panthers. The front-line Panther leadership is now either in jail or facing a long stretch in jail, and the party itself is having to devote much of its energy to this rather than to becoming a viable black political party.

The Panthers gave us the word "pig." They have preached the necessity of the gun. They, like Carmichael, have become a force, but primarily on the basis of image, rhetoric, and Eldridge Cleaver. Much of this rhetoric has been good. Much of the rhetoric has served to heighten the consciousness of the black radical movement and black people in general. But much of the rhetoric has been of therapeutic value only to those in need of therapy. One can understand and feel the anger which gives rise to the cry of "Free Huey or the sky's the limit!" But on the level of revolutionary strategy it makes little sense. One never tells the enemy what he is going to do. If the Vietnamese had told the French, "Get out of Vietnam or we will crush you at Dienbienphu," the French would've merely gotten out of Dienbienphu. But the Vietnamese didn't even bother speaking to the French. They spoke to the Vietnamese by sending out cadres into every area where there were Vietnamese and they organized, educated, propagandized, and acted.

Cleaver's recent speech in which he is reported to have called Governor Ronald Reagan a faggot and challenged him to a duel is too reminiscent of Carmichael's calling President Johnson a fool. It is difficult to see how such utterances will advance the struggle. Their only value is as entertainment. That, however, is not the business at hand.

The black radical movement is repeating itself. The media extract personalities from its ranks and give them enough publicity to make them "leaders." These "leaders" get caught up in the glamour of their own image. "The movement" is advanced for a while because of what these "leaders" articulate, but the point of diminishing returns is soon reached and "the movement" comes to a stop while it yet appears to be in motion. Meanwhile the enemy sneaks in quietly from the rear and redirects the energy which has been released. He takes the rhetoric and bends it to his ends. He provides a program and money and black power becomes respectable. Meanwhile the "leaders" are denouncing the enemy and the enemy is organizing the people.

History need not repeat itself. Hopefully the next potential black leader will immerse himself totally in the revolutionary process, and in so doing, realize that the transmitters of revolution are people organized around a program and strategy. SNCC did it in the South in the early 1960's. That, however, is a bit of history which has not repeated itself.

No matter how easy it may seem, one cannot use the media to one's own ends. Whatever gains are made are ultimately illusory. In present-day America the media can be nothing but an enemy of revolution. And they definitely cannot be used as a substitute for revolutionary analysis, theory, program, and strategy.

NOVEMBER 23, 1968

## JEWISH RACISM AND BLACK ANTI-SEMITISM

THE New York City school strike has ended, leaving a residue of ill feeling like few events in New York have done in recent years. The United Federation of Teachers claimed "due process" had been violated when the Ocean Hill-Brownsville governing board transferred the eighty-three teachers from the district. At issue was the extent to which the governing board could exercise the power to determine who was going to teach in the schools of the district. There can be no real community control if the community cannot have the power to decide who is going to teach in its schools.

Despite whatever liberal pretensions the UFT may make of being concerned about the education of children, it is a labor union whose overwhelming concern is the rights of its members. It is fond of proving its liberalism by pointing out that it played a role in the freedom schools in Mississippi in 1964 and that its president, Albert Shanker, participated in the Selma-Montgomery march and in the march in Memphis in support of the garbage workers' strike following the death of Martin Luther King. But it is usually easier for northern liberals to empathize with southern blacks than it is for them to do something about the problems in their own area. In other words, the UFT can be paternalistic like all other unions and racist when the problems come home to roost.

The issues involved in the school strike were almost immediately obscured when the UFT leveled charges of anti-Semitism against Ocean Hill. Unfortunately the predominantly Jewish UFT rank and file fell for the charge, as did a significant portion of New York's Jewish community. They believed the anti-Semitism charge despite the fact that 50 per cent of the teachers at Ocean Hill-Brownsville's Junior High School 271 (the focal point of the controversy) were Jewish and many of them had been hired to replace the teachers (some Jewish) who had been transferred by the governing board. It was clear that the hysteria which arose was more a reflection of the hysterical than of black reality in Ocean Hill.

Just as whites are often afraid to oppose something blacks favor for fear of being called racists, blacks find themselves in the position of being called anti-Semitic if they oppose something in which a large number of Jews are involved. Political opposition to the State of Israel is invariably translated as anti-Semitism. Thus, practically anyone, black or white, who supported the governing board of Ocean Hill, was accused of anti-Semitism.

If the New York City school strike proved anything, it proved that racism within the ranks of the UFT is the problem, not black anti-Semitism. UFT president Albert Shanker was fond of speaking of "mob rule," "extremists," "militants." All of these were epithets for blacks and cannot be excused or explained away. Few Jewish leaders came forward to condemn Shanker's remarks, and those who did—such as Jewish Teachers in Support of Ocean Hill-Brownsville—were subjected to harassment and vilification by striking teachers.

The change of black anti-Semitism was spurious, particularly in light of such evidence as the fact that the schools in the Ocean Hill district were the only schools in New York City to hand out leaflets to students explaining Rosh Hashana and why it was a school holiday. Yet the charge of anti-Semitism was vigorously enunciated, and if Shanker and the UFT teachers are now hated by blacks, it is not because they are Jewish, but simply because they declared themselves to be enemies of black people.

When black parents want to involve themselves actively in the education of their children, it should be an occasion for exultation. The UFT teachers claim that they were for parent involvement in the schools, but their actions do not reflect what they say. It is impossible for blacks and many whites in New York City to feel anything except that the majority of teachers are opposed to any parent involvement in the schools. And all possibility of dialogue between parents and striking teachers is impossible as long as the teachers interpret opposition to their position as anti-Semitism.

The UFT charge of anti-Semitism was merely a cloak for the unbridling of a racism of which George Wallace would have been proud. The UFT played upon fears of a "black holocaust," and the resultant response by most whites and Jews revealed one more layer of racism for all who cared to see.

The lesson to be drawn should be clear for all blacks. Depend upon no one except your own. Assume that everyone else is the enemy until they prove differently. But don't be afraid to offer the hand of solidarity to those who have proved themselves. Those who did not go out on strike should be supported. They recognize that the schools belong to the community and have shown themselves to be willing to make that a reality.

Those who were duped by the lies of anti-Semitism should recognize that they have been duped. They will continue to be duped as long as they allow themselves to be stampeded into hysteria by demagogues like Shanker. And as long as they are dupes, they remain victims of the system. Their state of victimization, however, does not exclude them from being categorized as enemies.

NOVEMBER 30, 1968

# THE MOVEMENT AT THE END OF THE DECADE

NINETEEN SIXTY-EIGHT was the year in which the momentum of the past eight years reached a climax. From the first day of that year, everyone could feel that this year was the year for a series of confrontations which would expose the enemy more and more. Columbia, Chicago, the Black Panthers, and much more happened—and the enemy was exposed to those who were predisposed to look and some who were not.

Now 1969 has come. The enemy is exposed and no one seems to know quite what to do about it. Many of us are suffering from a mild "depression," which is perhaps nothing more than a momentary weariness of the spirit. But perhaps it isn't. For along with that depression has come a feeling of frustration which more and more is causing us to fight among ourselves, to squabble, to disintegrate into factions.

A lot happened last year and yet the empire still stands, with bombs bursting in air and the flag still there. Not only was Rome not built in a day, but it didn't decline in a day. It is one thing to expose the enemy in the streets of Chicago. It is another to destroy him. It is the former that much of our activity and thought have been concerned with. It is the latter we must be concerned with now.

"The movement" has reached a critical stage. It must move from an action-oriented movement which was, in the main, concerned with single issues, (the war and/or the universities) to a broad-based, multi-level movement which will change the political and ecomomic structure of the country. Whether or not this particular "movement" with its myriad groups, attitudes, and viewpoints can do so is uncertain. It may be that we have done all that it was possible to do at this point in history, given who we were and where we came from. If that, however, is to be the fate of the organizations now existing, it must not be the fate of a significant minority of individuals who have been involved during the past eight years. However, even those individuals who have a total commitment will be caught in the backwash of frustration now upon us if there isn't a serious understanding of the job before us.

Many became involved in "the movement" because of their outrage over the war in Vietnam. Once involved, they slowly became aware of the many ways in which they were oppressed. Their involvement in "the movement" brought about changes within themselves and presented them with the possibility of an alternative life style. There is no doubt that the overwhelming majority of people who have been involved in "the movement" are better people for it and unfortunately, it is going to end there for so many. Having gotten from "the movement" what they needed, they will now leave "the movement," live better lives for having been involved, and become a part of that vast body which will form the liberals of tomorrow.

At the same time, however, there are those whose involvement is total. They have reached that point where the pain of others has become their own and they have no choice but to continue unto death or victory. It is upon them that the responsibilty falls to create what does not now exist—a revolutionary movement. For them, many dangers exist. As the numbers in "the movement" dwindle, they will become more exposed, on one hand, and more isolated, on the other. They may find themselves increasingly frustrated and discouraged as this situation develops. The experience may make them bitter, and embittered people do not make good revolutionaries.

The question is being asked: What do we do in 1969? Unless one asks the right questions, one cannot get the right answers, and the question is: What do we do, what do we want to achieve, what can we achieve, between now and 1972? After that question is answered, one tries to answer the question of what we do in 1969. For that minority of people who are committed, perhaps the overriding necessity for the next four years is to broaden the base of "the movement." This means developing a cadre of organizers and then moving in groups of two or three into various medium-sized cities (100,000-250,000) long enough to know the problems and learn what the possibilities are for long-range organizing (which does not necessarily mean organizing people for demonstrations). Cities of this size can be organized. The metropolitan areas can only be harassed. They will fall from their sheer weight when the time comes.

Another necessity which should be on the list for the

next four years is working and living in working-class communities. Labor will undoubtedly be in an accelerating crisis in the next four years, particularly if the Nixon administration carries through on its statement to increase unemployment to hold down inflation. It is a mistake to think that the working classes don't know where it's at. They do. They just don't know how to deal with it, except by consuming. And it is quite clear that the tactics we have used up to now haven't convinced them that we know how to deal with it, either. As long as we deal only with the particulars of our own type of oppression, they will find us irrelevant. We can be relevant to them only when we know their oppression.

Perhaps some of the motion for breaking down the class barriers of "the movement" will come from the women's liberation movement, one of the most significant developments of the past year. Women comprise the largest oppressed minority in the country. Any relevant political action coming from women can have much the same devastating effect on the country that the black movement has had. As prices continue to rise, it is not pipe-dreaming to think of women sending bricks through supermarket windows.

During the past eight years we have so often depended upon the enemy to keep our "movement" going. Now it is up to us. And that means developing a movement which has leaders, not personalities; theory, not rhetoric; strategy beyond demonstrations. We must realize that no one blow will topple the empire. It will take hundreds of thousands of little ones. That can happen only when we consciously make each of our acts relate to furthering the revolution. This means everything from the way you say good morning to how you plan to rob a bank to finance your organization. In the revolutionary, the personal life and the political life merge and become one.

Above all, we must not feel that we are not successful if we do not repeat 1968. The year 1968 had its own demands. The year 1969 has different ones. Let us take what we can use from 1968 and leave the rest. This is 1969 and the empire still stands. That means there is work to be done.

JANUARY 4, 1969

## THE CULTURAL WORKER IN THE REVOLUTION

OF necessity, much of the black and white radical movements have been involved in a cultural revolution. For blacks it has led to an affirmation of blackness, an affirmation of self, for I must know who I am before I can know that I cannot be destroyed. For young whites, the cultural revolution has been a process of creating psychic liberation zones which embody the seeds of new values and new attitudes. A man cannot begin to be involved in the revolutionary process until he looks at himself, and thereby others, with new feelings and new ideas. The cultural revolution has been a dominant factor in this.

At the same time, however, it has to be realized that the cultural revolution can serve only as a part of the foundation upon which the revolution will be built. Unfortunately many blacks, now in intimate contact with their blackness, act as if they had achieved the final goal. Many whites have become ensconced in their psychic liberation zones and are involved in trying to create institutions to preserve and protect their psyches. But as Rap Brown has pointed out, it's not possible to beat "the man" to death with your daishiki. And "the man" is not about to be asphyxiated from the smoke of a stick of "grass." The means has become the end for all too many.

Last week *The Guardian* published a twelve-page special supplement on Cuba. This supplement concerned itself with the many aspects of Cuban culture and, in and of itself, had great value. Nonetheless, when considered in the context of the movement here and what it can learn from Cuba, the supplement was a reflection of Western intellectuals trying to be revolutionary and not succeeding.

Culture in a revolutionary context must be an instrument of communication, which serves to raise political awareness and consciousness, as well as serving to further intensify the commitment of the people to revolution. Culture can also be an instrument which serves as a rock in a weary land and a shelter in a time of storm. Culture is the principal mass means by which attitudes and ideology are shaped in any society. Therefore, in a revolutionary context, the responsibilities of the cultural worker are overwhelming. These responsibilities have different demands at different stages of the revolution, and it is part of the cultural worker's responsibility to be so attuned to the needs of the revolution that he will not be articulating one thing when another is needed.

However, it is difficult for intellectuals and artists to make that change whereby they become cultural workers. As intellectuals and artists, there is a necessary and constant need to be concerned with form, i.e., how best to say what is said. In the Western intellectual-artist, this has often led to an almost exclusive concern with form over content. The revolutionary artist, of course, becomes counterrevolutionary when a concern with form overwhelms that which is to be communicated. In revolutionary societies, cultural workers are sometimes required to work in factories or in the fields so that they will learn in the very marrow of their bones what needs to be communicated and to whom (because intellectuals and artists have overwhelming tendencies to become their own best audiences).

In our society the intellectual-artist who wishes to use his skills in a revolutionary context has a fiendishly difficult job, because in most instances he must provide his own political direction. There is no revolutionary party or organization which is presently giving the intellectual-artist the necessary framework in which he can use his skills. (Emory Douglas, revolutionary artist and minister of culture of the Black Panthers, is a notable exception.) Thus the intellectual-artist operates as best he can within the context of the cultural revolution, which has its own dynamic, a dynamic which is not necessarily revolutionary.

There is much the intellectual-artist can learn from the Cuban culture of today as he begins that journey to becoming a cultural worker. Yet the fact still remains that Cuban culture exists in the framework of a revolutionary society, not in the framework of an incipient revolutionary movement which has still to win its first battle. Thus, the demands made on the cultural worker inside the movement are entirely different from those made on the Cuban cultural worker, who has the support and encouragement of the state. It would have been more worthwhile if *The Guardian* had examined the role of culture in the struggle of the Viet Minh against the French, the National Liberation Front against the U.S., the role of culture in the Cuban fight against the U.S., the role of culture in the guerrilla struggles in Mozambique, Portuguese Guinea, and other places in Africa. The intellectual-artist of the movement can best identify and learn from the intellectual-artist of other struggling movements. *The Guardian* supplement, while containing valuable concepts and ideas, still has the end effect of making you wish you were in Cuba, where it is easier to be a cultural worker.

If *The Guardian* wished to commemorate the tenth anniversary of the revolution, it would've been more valuable to have printed twelve pages of excerpts from the writings of José Martí, a Cuban who is one of the most important revolutionary intellectuals in the Western hemisphere, a man who lived in a prerevolutionary period and died in an unsuccessful attempt to take power. How did Martí deal with the psychological problems the revolutionary artist in a prerevolutionary period faces? Martí is a man practically unknown in the movement and remains one of the most important men to know, particularly for those who aspire to be cultural workers.

The Cuban cultural supplement was informative, but it could just have easily appeared in the *New York Times* Sunday magazine section. *The Guardian* sometimes reminds one of Omar Sharif in the role of Che, standing in front of the cameras, acting as he thinks a revolutionary acts, but not having the vaguest notion what it's all about. A twelve-page supplement on Cuba is not necessarily a revolutionary act. Too many people in the movement use a trip to Cuba as all the proof they need to be regarded as revolutionaries. A trip to Cuba proves only one thing: you went to Cuba. A twelve-page supplement in *The Guardian* on Cuba proves only that there was a twelve-page supplement in *The Guardian* on Cuba. Meanwhile, the intellectuals and artists in the movement still need that framework in which their skills can be put to use.

JANUARY 18, 1969

# MILITARY STRATEGY IN THE BLACK COMMUNITY

THE revolutionary process takes many decades to fulfill itself. The generation which finally assumes power gives the appearance of having started a revolution in a short period of time. That is not so. The generation which wins power is only completing work begun decades before.

The 1960's have been a decade of rapid change. Each succeeding year has seen a heightening of consciousness, and while problems exist in great abundance, these problems will be overcome if the organization, understanding, will, and discipline exist to do the necessary work to see that they are overcome. Each succeeding year of the 1960's has also seen an intensification of the actual struggle itself. The early willingness to suffer arrest and go to jail has given way to an attitude of "catch me if you can," not to mention the increasing willingness of people to fight back when attacked.

One of the most important changes in consciousness has been the acceptance of the concept of self-defense. When

Robert Williams organized self-defense units in Monroe, North Carolina, he eventually had to leave the country to save his life. Malcolm X brought the concept to a mass audience and was eventually killed. The Black Panthers have made the concept manifest on a mass level and are suffering intense harassment. But today there are no debates over the rightness of defending one's self and one's community.

The next step in the evolution of the revolutionary process will be the move from self-defense to aggressive action. This has occurred in a few isolated instances, particularly on college campuses on the West Coast and a few black campuses, where buildings have been set afire and heavily damaged. This type of activity will, in all likelihood, increase in the coming months.

The black community has settled down to a quiet state of low-key warfare. In New York and various communities in New Jersey there have been numerous attacks on police stations in the past few months. Though most of them have been unsuccessful, the mere fact that the attempts are being made is significant. The black movement has reached a point where it is unnecessary to discuss the necessity of "the gun" any longer. People know what needs to be done and are going about and doing it.

One city in the country which has settled down to a state of constant war is East St. Louis. The *St. Louis Post-Dispatch* of January 16 reports that since August, 1968, there have been more than fifty sniping incidents in East St. Louis. Three people have been killed in these incidents —an 18-year-old white boy and two white men shot in an after-hours tavern by a sniper firing from a bridge. The effect of "The Sniper" (there is probably more than one) on the economic life of the city has been profound. Because whites are now afraid even to drive through East St. Louis, sales tax revenues from the city to the state declined by $30,000 in the third quarter, which ended October 31. The mayor's office estimates that over-all, the sniper has cost the city $200,000 in sales taxes, merchants' license collections, and overtime pay for policemen. There is no estimate of how much revenue the city will lose by businesses leaving the area.

To the black community, "The Sniper" has become a hero. He is known to shoot only at whites or at blacks who are known enemies of the community. He is also known to be bold, able to strike at high noon or after midnight with equal impunity.

The number of fires in the East St. Louis-St. Louis area has also increased. These fires seem generally to be directed against white businesses known to be cruelly exploitative in the community. Firemen now carry rifles as part of their standard equipment, which gives an indication of just how serious the situation has become. Police have been totally ineffective in dealing with "The Sniper" or those who are sabotaging the businesses.

What is happening in East St. Louis points up once again the advantages of medium-sized cities. In the large cities of the East and West, the police have tremendous sophistication and are much more difficult to combat. In the medium-sized cities of the South and Midwest, this is not true to the same extent. The military parallel of this is the Vietnam war, where the National Liberation Front has concentrated on small and medium-sized cities, leaving

Saigon, Danang, and other large cities for the last. And in fact the same practice prevailed in the revolutionary wars in China and Cuba. This is not to say that the large cities should be ignored. They cannot be. But the risks are higher, the preparation needed much greater, and unless the action taken is a large one, the returns from the action might be smaller than if the action were taken in a smaller city.

On the surface it may appear that the black movement is in a state of disarray. While this may be partially true of some groups, the black movement has never been isolated from the black community. In an unorganized sense, the community has been the military wing of the movement, while known groups have been the political wing. Some theoreticians of the white radical movement considered the black rebellions of 1965-68 to be nonrevolutionary in content because they were aimed at property, which thereby made them "consumer-oriented."

This kind of analysis points up once again how at variance the black and white radical movements are. Having been glutted by a consumer-oriented society, it is natural that young whites fight against it. Having been on the outside, it is natural that blacks would seek to acquire. What the white radical theoreticians overlook is the way in which blacks have done their acquiring and the subsequent destruction of property that inevitably comes after the acquisitions have been made. The black rebellions also served as "on-the-job" training for what is now developing in East St. Louis, and no doubt other cities around the country.

If East St. Louis is any indication, the revolutionary process has entered another stage. At present, it is harassing action. Undoubtedly, it will be followed by terrorist action in the white community, and eventually all-out guerrilla warfare. It is to be hoped that the white radical movement will be able to relate effectively to what is developing in the black community.

JANUARY 25, 1969

# SELF-CRITICISM

ONE of the most difficult responsibilities of the revolutionary is to be self-critical. To be self-critical means being able to ask yourself if you are wrong and, if so, to admit the fact and correct it. Revolutionary self-criticism also involves the necessity to see mistakes before they actually happen and, thus, avoid them. However, to engage in self-criticism affords no guarantee that errors will be avoided or corrected. Self-criticism can lead to its own mistakes. The only thing the revolutionary knows for sure is that poverty, exploitation in all of its infinite varieties, and racism must be destroyed. It is the question of "how" which involves the revolutionary and the concomitant responsibility to be self-critical.

The movement has reached an important plateau where the question of "how" echoes through every meeting, rally, demonstration, and conversation. And it is to the long-range answer of this question that attention must now be turned. To say armed struggle is to say little except the obvious.

It is the tracks upon which the revolution must travel. But what the design of the train will be, how many cars it should be composed of, and exactly what fuel the train will use are some of the questions which must be answered.

For somewhat more than a year, this column has appeared in *The Guardian* and other newspapers around the country. During that time it has sought to raise questions, answer questions, and present the viewpoint of one black individual involved in the revolutionary process. More often than not, these columns have reflected the thinking of a poet rather than a theoretician, which is not to denigrate whatever value the columns may have had, but simply to define them and to understand what their function has been.

The writer of a weekly column, if he aspires to be a revolutionary, is soon faced with the overwhelming problem of trying to say something relevant and meaningful each and every week. That is the revolutionary's responsibility—to let every word and every act, political and personal, be fraught with meaning, meaning which will further the revolutionary process. Such a responsibility is almost too much for any single individual. Yet it is the responsibility each of us has.

At the same time, a writer may find himself faced with the problem of people responding so completely to what he writes that they look upon him as an oracle, a symbol, a model. This is, perhaps, unavoidable, but it places upon that writer an even more immense responsibility. If what he says affects people to some degree, he, in turn, becomes partially responsible for those people. The writer cannot turn from that responsibility. Neither can he mistake the people's bestowing of this responsibility upon him as a means of self-aggrandizement. The only result of this will be an ego trip into increasing irrelevance.

In attempting to shoulder his responsibility, the writer must always be aware of when he has something to say and when he doesn't. The greatest danger comes when he has nothing to say, but continues to speak because it is expected of him. But the words that are not written are as much, if not more, a part of writing than the words which are written.

When this column began, it tried to speak to the asked and unasked questions in people's minds. A year and some months later, new questions face us. Those questions must and will be answered by the movement. Whatever role this writer might be able to play in the search for the right answers cannot be fulfilled at the present time if the necessity to write a column each and every week continues. This is not a sudden decision, but one reached after some three months of intense questioning. How long this column will be absent is uncertain. Perhaps it will never return.

There is much that we don't know. In fact, our ignorance is greater than our knowledge, which means that there is much study and much work to be done. Just as the revolutionary artists and writers of Cuba and China find it necessary to go to the fields and factories to work and live, this writer finds that he can best fulfill his responsibilities at the present time by working in the fields to combat his own ignorance in each of its manifestations.

The revolution proceeds not by steps of a league at a time, but slowly—painfully slowly—and its steps are often so small as to be unnoticeable. The revolution proceeds not by the speeches at the barricades, but from one person to another person, in conversation and in work. The revolution proceeds not at the pace of our desires, but by its own laws. To break down the old and build the new is not a task accomplished in one generation or several, or by one individual more than another. It is accomplished only when each feels as responsible for the other as he does himself and acts in accordance with that responsibility.

We have reached a plateau. Some have started the excruciating climb to the next. Others have need of new supplies and new materials before they can begin. The face of the mountain is rough and complex, and, in many places, is totally unknown. Each has a job to do and each has to prepare.

So be it.

FEBRUARY 1, 1969

# INDEX